*access to history*

# Indian Independence 1914–64

TIM LEADBEATER

## SECOND EDITION

HODDER
EDUCATION
AN HACHETTE UK COMPANY

The Publishers would like to thank Robin Bunce and Sarah Ward for their contributions to the Study Guide.

The Publishers would like to thank the following for permission to reproduce copyright material:

**Photo credits: p6** Miss Wheeler defending herself against Sepoys at Cawnpore in 1857, from 'The History of the Indian Mutiny', published in 1858 (engraving), English School, (19th century)/Private Collection/Ken Welsh/Bridgeman Images; **p29** Eduard Thony/ Mary Evans Picture Library; **p32** Kent Cartoon Archive/Solo Syndication ; **p40** https://commons.wikimedia.org/wiki/File:Portrait_ Gandhi.jpg; **p53** Topham Picturepoint; **p63** Douglas Miller/Getty Images; **p69** https://en.wikipedia.org/wiki/File:Quaid6_edited.jpg; **p84** Library of Congress, 3c11781; **p89** Paul Popper/Popperfoto/Getty Images; **pp91, 99** National Library of Wales/Solo Syndication; **p110** Library of Congress, LC-USZ62-98953; **p111** Topfoto; **p128** Bettmann/Corbis; **p129** Kent Cartoon Archive/Solo Syndication; **p143** https://commons.wikimedia.org/wiki/File:Jnehru.jpg; **p155** Larry Burrows/The LIFE Picture Collection/Getty Images.

**Acknowledgements:** B.W. Huebsch, *Young India 1919–1922* by Mahatma Gandhi, 1924. Cambridge University Press, *The Empire Project: The Rise and Fall of the British World-System, 1830–1970* by John Darwin, 2009. Chatto & Windus, *Divide and Quit: An Eyewitness Account of the Partition of India* by Penderel Moon, 1961. Flamingo, *Liberty or Death* by Patrick French, 1997. *Hansard*, HL Deb, 26 February 1924, volume 56, columns 320–62. Her Majesty's Stationery Office, *Indian Statutory Commission Report*, volume 2, Cmd 3569, 1930; *Parliamentary Papers X: India and the War* (1939–40), Cmd 6196, 1940; *Report of Committee Appointed to Investigate the Disturbances in the Punjab*, Cmd 681 by William Hunter, 1920; *The Report on Indian Constitutional Reforms*, Cmd 9109, 1918. Houghton Mifflin Harcourt, *The Hinge of Fate* by Winston S. Churchill, 1986. India Office, Harry Haig Papers, India Office Library, London. Konark Publishing, *Secret Papers from British Royal Archives* by P.N. Chopra, Prabha Chopra and Padmsha Jha, 1998. Little, Brown & Co., *Raj: The Making and Unmaking of British India* by Lawrence James, 1997. Macmillan, *Indian Unrest* by Valentine Chirol, 1910. Macmillan, *The Indian Nationalist Movement 1885–1947: Select Documents* by B.N. Pandey, editor, 1979. Nehru Memorial Museum and Library, Nehru Papers. Nehru Memorial Museum and Library, T.B. Sapru Papers. Orient Blackswan, *The Rediscovery of India: A New Subcontinent* by Ansar Hussain Khan, 1999. Orient Longman, *Transfer of Power in India* by V.P. Menon, 1957. Oxford University Press, *A Dictionary of Modern Indian History 1707–1947* by P. Mehra, 1987; *Modern India: The Origins of an Asian Democracy* by Judith Brown, 1994; *India's Partition* by Mushirul Hasan, editor, 1994; *Jinnah of Pakistan* by Stanley Wolpert, 1984; *Jinnah of Pakistan* by Stanley Wolpert, 1984; *Shameful Flight, The Last Years of the British Empire in India* by Stanley Wolpert, 2006; *The Great Divide* by H.V. Hodson, 1985. Penguin, *Nehru* by M.J. Akbar, 1989. Scolar Press, *The District Officer in India, 1930–1947* by Roland Hunt and John Harrison, 1980. Theosophical Publishing Society, *The Thirty-Second Indian National Congress Calcutta*, 1917. Vikas Publishing, *Towards India's Freedom and Partition* by S.R. Mehrotra, 1978.

Every effort has been made to trace all copyright holders, but if any have been inadvertently overlooked the Publishers will be pleased to make the necessary arrangements at the first opportunity.

Although every effort has been made to ensure that website addresses are correct at time of going to press, Hodder Education cannot be held responsible for the content of any website mentioned in this book. It is sometimes possible to find a relocated web page by typing in the address of the home page for a website in the URL window of your browser.

Hachette UK's policy is to use papers that are natural, renewable and recyclable products and made from wood grown in sustainable forests. The logging and manufacturing processes are expected to conform to the environmental regulations of the country of origin.

Orders: please contact Bookpoint Ltd, 130 Milton Park, Abingdon, Oxon OX14 4SB. Telephone: +44 (0)1235 827720. Fax: +44 (0)1235 400454. Lines are open 9.00a.m.–5.00p.m., Monday to Saturday, with a 24-hour message answering service. Visit our website at www.hoddereducation.co.uk

Cover photo © Mary Evans Picture Library
Produced, illustrated and typeset in Palatino LT Std by Gray Publishing, Tunbridge Wells
Printed and bound by CPI Group (UK) Ltd, Croydon CR0 4YY

A catalogue record for this title is available from the British Library

**ISBN 978 1471838125**

# Contents

## Dedication

**Keith Randell (1943–2002)**

The *Access to History* series was conceived and developed by Keith, who created a series to 'cater for students as they are, not as we might wish them to be'. He leaves a living legacy of a series that for over 20 years has provided a trusted, stimulating and well-loved accompaniment to post-16 study. Our aim with these new editions is to continue to offer students the best possible support for their studies.

## CHAPTER 1

# Context: India to 1914

In 1914 India was part of the British Empire but by the end of 1947 India had gained independence. This chapter sets out the context of the nationalist movement for independence. The nineteenth century witnessed the most troubled and then the most confident time for the British Raj (rule). British territorial control was at its greatest and treaties were negotiated with the Indian rulers of hundreds of independent states, forcing them to acknowledge Britain's supreme authority. After a mutiny in 1857–8, radical changes were made to the government of India.

This chapter examines:

★ The Indian subcontinent before 1914

★ The Indian Mutiny

★ The British Raj

★ Imperialism and the growth of nationalism

## Key dates

| | | | |
|---|---|---|---|
| 1526–1707 | Height of Mughal dynasty | 1877 | Queen Victoria declared empress |
| 1600 | Charter granted to East India Company by Elizabeth I | 1885 | Formation of Congress Party |
| | | 1905 | Partition of Bengal |
| 1857 | Indian Mutiny began | 1906 | Formation of Muslim League |
| 1858 | Crown control of India; Royal Proclamation | 1907 | Congress split |
| | | 1909 | Morley–Minto reforms and Indian Councils Act |
| 1875 | Foundation of Aligarh College | | |

# 1 The Indian subcontinent before 1914

▶ *To what extent had India been a unified country before 1914?*

The land of pre-independent India covers an area equivalent to Europe and is often referred to as the South Asian subcontinent. The population in 1914 was about 350 million, speaking some 200 languages. In the era before technology, uniting and controlling such a vast country was next to impossible. Between 1600 and 1900 the British had established control over large areas but not all. There were still nearly 600 Indian princes, each ruling their own state.

**Punjab** A fertile and densely populated region in the north-west, with its own language and culture but now split between India and Pakistan. The name comes from *panch* (five) *ab* (rivers), so often it is also written Panjab.

**Communal** Relating to religious groups in India.

**Polytheistic** A religion with many gods and goddesses.

**Caste** A rigid public social division. Derived from a Portuguese word. The English word outcast is related.

The most significant region is the Indo-Gangetic river plain, an arc up the Ganges from Bengal, across the **Punjab** and down the Indus. This highly populated region has been settled and farmed since prehistory and has been the territorial base of almost all the rulers of India. Both Calcutta, the former British capital, and Delhi, the medieval and modern capital, lie within the arc. This cosmopolitan and diverse area was the centre of political reform movements in the late nineteenth century.

## Indian society and religion

Religious sensitivities and tensions run through the entire history of British rule and the nationalist campaigns. The relations between religious groups are referred to as **communal** politics. Before independence, Hindus were the predominant Indian religious group, with significant groups of Muslims and Sikhs in particular regions.

### Hindus

The Hindu religion, one of the oldest in the world, is **polytheistic**. One's relationship with a god or goddess is less important than public behaviour, religious duties and social responsibilities appropriate to one's socio-religious group. Such groups are called **castes**.

Caste membership, which is largely determined by birth, determines which occupations may be followed, whom one might marry and even the extent to which one might simply appear in public.

Historically, there were four main castes:

- Brahmins, the priests
- Kshatriyas, the warriors
- Vaishyas, the traders
- Shudras, the cultivators or peasants.

The Brahmin class, proud, sensitive and powerless, was a focus for resentment of the British and later for educated resistance and organisation.

### The Untouchables

At the other end of the hierarchy, there was oppression of the lowest group, not even permitted a caste status and known as the Untouchables. The British refused to use this term and referred to the Depressed Classes (or the Scheduled Classes); the modern Indian term is Dalits.

### Muslims

The Muslim population of north-western India is the result of invasions by Turkic peoples from central Asia starting in the thirteenth century. From 1526 the Mughal dynasty conquered most of the subcontinent, but ruling only as a hegemonic minority elite. Mughal power began to decline after the long reign of Aurangzeb ended in 1707, shrinking again to a small state around Delhi.

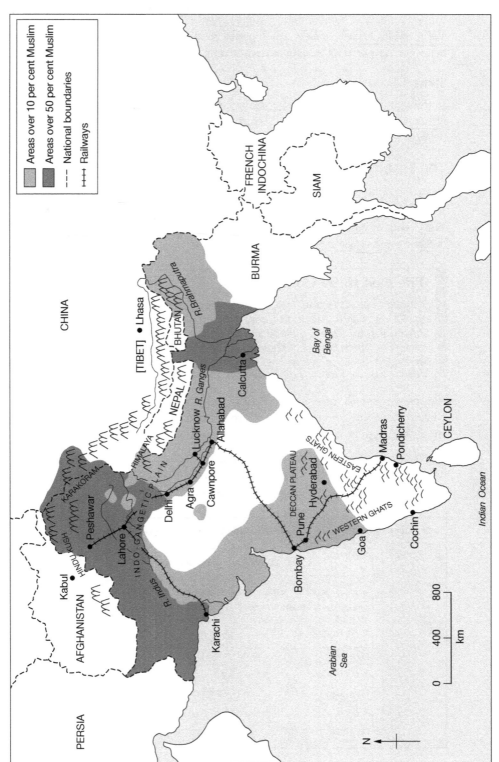

**Figure 1.1**  The Indian subcontinent, showing geographical and physical features, and proportions of Muslim people in the early twentieth century.

Legend:
- Areas over 10 per cent Muslim
- Areas over 50 per cent Muslim
- National boundaries
- Railways

In the Punjab and Bengal, many people converted to Islam to escape their low status in Hindu caste society. Islam places great emphasis on the equality of believers. As a result, these areas became majority Muslim regions.

### Sikhs

In the sixteenth century religious leaders in the Punjab created a fusion of Hinduism and Islam, known as Sikhism. Over time, the Punjab became overwhelmingly Sikh and Muslim with almost no Hindus.

## The East India Company

English (not British until the 1707 Act of Union) contact with India began in the reign of Elizabeth I, who granted a royal charter to the East India Company. The Company created and put into the field its own substantial private army, defeating and expelling the French from India in the eighteenth century.

> ### The East India Company
>
> This was a private company given a monopoly over the spice trade from the Pacific islands (East Indies, now Indonesia). It had three bases in India, initially just for restocking food and water, at Calcutta, Madras and Bombay. When the Dutch Empire ousted the British from the East Indies, the Company expanded its Indian operations. Its most successful general was Robert Clive.

Aggressive expansion resulted in British control of the entire Gangetic plain. Nevertheless, the Company professed to have no political objectives: it was simply trying to protect trade and capture (literally) more market.

The British saw themselves as the dominant power in India for the foreseeable future. Increasingly, their attitude displayed a **paternalistic** concern to spread the benefits of British civilisation and Christian culture.

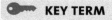

**KEY TERM**

**Paternalistic** The caring but superior attitude of a parent (specifically a father) who knows best.

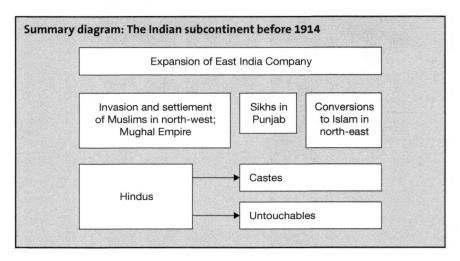

Summary diagram: The Indian subcontinent before 1914

- Expansion of East India Company
- Invasion and settlement of Muslims in north-west; Mughal Empire
- Sikhs in Punjab
- Conversions to Islam in north-east
- Hindus → Castes
- Hindus → Untouchables

#  The Indian Mutiny

▶ *What were the causes and effects of the Indian Mutiny?*

In 1857 hidden anger among Indians concerning Company rule erupted in what came to be known as the Indian Mutiny. It left deep scars and the thought of it happening again lurked in the collective British memory for the rest of British control right up to independence.

## Causes

The key causes of the mutiny were reactions to British policies and interventions:

- **annexation** of Indian states when the ruler died without an heir
- Brahmin opposition to railways because of the possibilities for religious pollution by coming into contact, literally, with Untouchables
- Brahmin **sepoy** opposition to deployments outside their home region and overseas, which were regarded as disrespectful.

The final spark which ignited rebellion was the rumour that ammunition cartridges issued by the British to sepoys for their rifles had been greased for easier loading (which involved tearing off part of the cartridge with the mouth) with either beef fat, sacred to Hindus, or pork fat, prohibited by Islam.

## Key events in the mutiny

The key events were as follows:

- Eighty-five sepoys were **court-martialled** at the barracks in Meerut, near Delhi, for refusing to use the cartridges. They were freed by mutineers, who on the same night massacred all local Europeans, including women and children.
- The mutiny spread rapidly throughout the Bengal Army of northern India and the entire Gangetic plain quickly fell out of British control. The mutineers marched on Delhi and made the 82-year-old Mughal 'emperor' ruler of all India.
- In the town of Cawnpore, 400 British men, women and children surrendered and were offered safe passage on boats. On their way to the boats they were massacred.

## Consequences

The consequences of the mutiny included the following:

- British reprisals, deliberately designed to strike terror into the peasant population. Entire villages were massacred by the British; thousands were bayoneted. Mutineers and others were forced to try to lick clean the blood-stained buildings, before being made to eat pork or beef, and then publicly hanged.

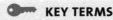

> **KEY TERMS**
>
> **Annexation** Forced but peaceful conquest of territory.
>
> **Sepoy** An Indian soldier.
>
> **Court-martialled** Punished by a military court for breach of army regulations, desertion and so on.

- The conclusion that a slow response had been disastrous. The fear of repeating this apparent mistake was, however, to have even more devastating consequences in the Amritsar Massacre of 1919 (see page 29).
- The British were determined to bring the administration of India under closer government control.

**SOURCE A**

A contemporary engraving of Ulrica Wheeler (aged eighteen years) defending herself during the Indian Mutiny, published in a popular book. Miss Wheeler was thought to have died; however, there is evidence that she lived a full but disguised life as the Muslim wife of one of her attackers or rescuers.

? What feelings might an image like Source A have aroused in British readers at the time?

**Summary diagram: The Indian Mutiny**

| Causes | Effects |
| --- | --- |
| • Annexations<br>• Caste pollution on rail transport<br>• Disrespect through overseas deployment<br>• Offence at greased cartridges | • Immediate terrorising reprisals<br>• Long-term fear of repeat: letting events get out of hand<br>• Closer government control |

#  The British Raj

▶ *Why and how did the British reorganise the governance of India?*

In the aftermath of the mutiny, the British took official control of India. In 1858 → *Royal Proclamation*
the East India Company was abolished and the British monarch, Queen Victoria,
became the ruler of India. From 1877 India was declared an empire in itself
under the Queen-Empress. The Governor General took the title of **Viceroy**.

🔑 **KEY TERM**

**Viceroy** The deputy for a monarch.

In 1858 the Queen issued a Royal Proclamation which included promises to
admit suitably educated Indians into the administration of Indian government
and this promise led to the involvement of Indians at all levels in the
administration.

## Structure of government in 1914

The governance of British India retained the structure set up in the aftermath of
the mutiny, as set out in Figure 1.2 on page 8:

- Responsibility for Indian affairs rested with the secretary of state for India, a
  member of the cabinet and accountable to Parliament, who was advised by
  the India Council.
- In India itself, the viceroy was supreme, the representative of the monarch but
  appointed by the prime minister and accountable to the secretary of state. The
  personal and political relationship of these two post-holders – viceroy and
  secretary of state – was crucial to the initiation, or not, of constitutional and
  political developments in and for India.
- Although technological progress meant that by 1914 telegraphic
  communication between London and India was relatively quick and easy, the
  viceroy had considerable powers of delegated government and, in states of
  emergency, absolute power.
- The viceroy had a military commander-in-chief in India and was advised by a
  national Legislative Council, overwhelmingly composed of British officials.
- The eleven British provinces had governors, advised by provincial councils,
  although only certain matters were permitted for discussion and decision.
- The Indian Civil Service (ICS) comprised about 2000 administrators for a
  population of 350 million, backed up by 60,000 British soldiers and 200,000
  Indians, less than one soldier for every 1000 Indians.

## The princely states

Many areas of the subcontinent were still not ruled directly by the British.
About one-fifth of the population, 72 million people, were the subjects of the
561 Indian rulers, some Hindu, some Muslim, with various titles such as Rajah,
Nawab or Nizam, but known collectively as the Indian princes.

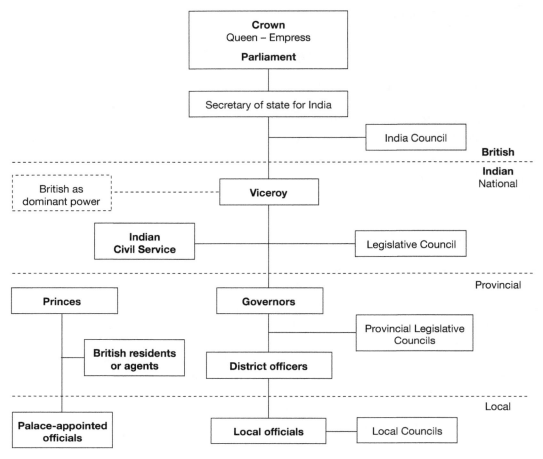

Figure 1.2 Governance of British India from 1857 to 1947.

The princes ruled nominally independent states (originally styled 'native' states and then 'princely' states), which varied considerably in size. Some states, such as Hyderabad in the south or Jammu and Kashmir in the north-west (c.200,000 km² each), were larger than Britain itself. Others were so small they were more like country estates and could not be found on maps.

After the mutiny, the British stopped acquiring territory either by military force or by political annexation. They permitted the Indian princes to continue to rule, partly as a reward for loyalty during the mutiny and partly to save more direct expense by the government.

On the other hand, the princely states were forced to acknowledge Britain as the **paramount power** within the subcontinent. This too was typically sweetened as a treaty guaranteeing British military protection. However, the British reserved, and sometimes exercised, the right to remove a prince found to be working against the British interest or causing trouble with neighbouring princes.

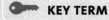 **KEY TERM**

**Paramount power**
A diplomatic term for the most powerful force, often an occupying army.

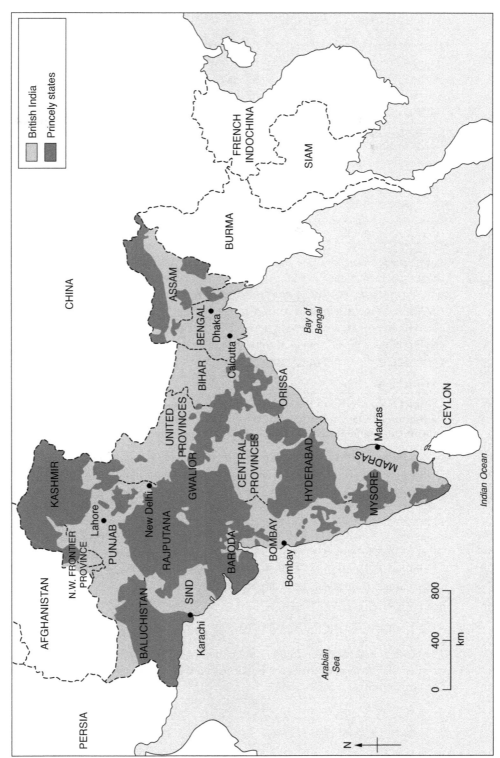

**Figure 1.3** India c.1914 showing British provinces and major princely states.

## The partition of Bengal

The province of Bengal contained a population of 78 million people, twice as large as Britain's. It was also prone to unrest as a growing middle class, educated by the British and ambitious, was still squeezed out of the ICS. In 1905 only five per cent of the ICS was Indian. Calcutta was both the provincial capital and the seat of British Indian government. After its formation in 1885 the nationalist Congress Party (see page 14) grew successfully in Bengal. The viceroy, **Lord Curzon**, decided that the province should be partitioned and intended to use a policy of **divide and rule** (see Source B). → Bengal

Despite a complete lack of formal consultation with Indians, two new provinces were created in 1905: Western Bengal with 42 million Hindus and 9 million Muslims; and Eastern Bengal with 12 million Hindus and 18 million Muslims.

The **partition** created a precedent for the reorganisation of territory and government along religious lines. The Bengali Hindus were outraged because the partition cut right through the unity of the Bengali-speaking community in order to create a majority Muslim province with equal status. In the short term, the Muslims were delighted with their majority in the new eastern province. This would provide them with a power base if and when Indians were able to elect provincial governments. Congress launched a campaign of *swadesh*, in particular against Lancashire cotton, which was publicly burned.

### SOURCE B

**Extract from a letter to the secretary of state from Viceroy Curzon, dated 2 February 1905, quoted in John Darwin, *The Empire Project: The Rise and Fall of the British World-System, 1830–1970*, Cambridge University Press, 2009, p. 204.**

*Calcutta is the centre from which the Congress Party is manipulated throughout the whole of Bengal and indeed the whole of India … the whole of their activity is directed to creating an agency so powerful that they may one day be able to force a weak government to give them what they desire. Any measure in consequence that would divide the Bengali-speaking population; that would permit independent centres of activity and influence to grow up; that would dethrone Calcutta from its place as the centre of successful intrigue or that would weaken the lawyer class, who have the entire organisation in their hands, is intensely and hotly resented by them.*

## The Indian Councils Act 1909

The government had been caught out by the Bengal agitation and the support for *swadesh*. It was aware that the public feared the unrest might spark off another mutiny.

Lord Morley, secretary of state of the new Liberal government in Britain (1906), proposed an increase of Indian involvement in its own government. There were no geographical constituencies as in British politics. Representatives would be elected from within the various Indian communities.

The Morley–Minto Reforms, as they are frequently termed, became law as the Indian Councils Act 1909. The Act resulted in a small number of elected members, including Indians, being added to the Legislative Councils at all levels of government.

The stated purpose of the reform was to bring in a cross-section of public opinion and this could only be guaranteed by reserving numbers of seats for specified groups. For the first time, council seats were reserved distinctively for Muslims, among other social groups, such as universities. Not only that, but a principle of weightage was applied to make the minority groups larger than they would be if strictly proportionate to population numbers. This was a crucial precedent.

Having granted Muslims separate electorates, the British felt able to balance this in 1911 with a reversal of the partition of Bengal which had created a Muslim-majority province. This placated Hindus but profoundly disappointed Muslims, although they were pleased at the simultaneous transfer of the capital of British India from Calcutta, the East India Company city, to Delhi, the historic Mughal capital.

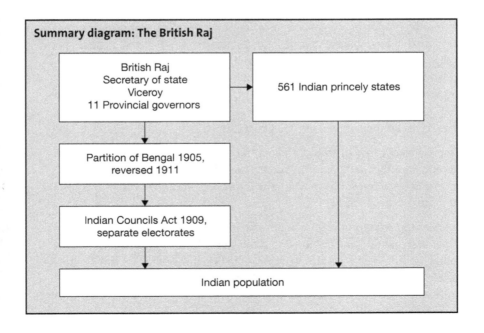

Summary diagram: The British Raj

- British Raj
  Secretary of state
  Viceroy
  11 Provincial governors
- 561 Indian princely states
- Partition of Bengal 1905, reversed 1911
- Indian Councils Act 1909, separate electorates
- Indian population

# Imperialism and the growth of nationalism

▶ *What were the different attitudes to independence?*

▶ *How did British and Indian attitudes towards each other develop in the late nineteenth century?*

At the start of the twentieth century the British Empire was the largest in world history and the Raj in India was often referred to as the 'Jewel in the Crown'. However, by 1914 there were signs of a nationalist movement to prepare Indians for the idea of self-government.

## Imperialism

The British Empire was just one of a number of European empires then at their height. The French, Belgians, Germans and Italians together with the British had all scrambled for parts of Africa and, nearer to home, the Austro-Hungarian and **Ottoman Empires** remained solid. All had difficulties with local peoples and politics but there was no sense that imperialism as a global system would disappear.

### The importance of India to Britain

Official British policy was commitment to eventual Indian self-government within the Empire but it was seen as a lengthy project of many decades. The sheer size and symbolism of India as a 'possession' of the British made it indispensable to British power and prestige around the globe. In addition, the Indian Army was a huge military force at its disposal in Asia. A new strategic importance of India was its role in resisting southward expansion of the Russian Empire and, to a lesser extent, the Chinese. Spying and skirmishes in the Himalayas became known as 'The Great Game'.

Empires were costly to protect and maintain but they provided access to vast resources for the manufacturing industries in Britain, whose goods were then sold back to colonial markets, with the imperial government extracting taxes at all stages of the process.

Socially, the British ~~shouldered willingly the so-called~~ *believed in the* **white man's burden** of passing on European culture and civilisation. Such a responsibility was, of course, self-defined and self-justifying. One British leader described it, rather tastelessly, as 'splendid happy slavery'. In practice, however, the educated but underemployed Bengali elite had time on its hands to imagine a different way of governing India.

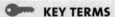

### KEY TERMS

**Ottoman Empire** Islamic Empire of the Middle East and modern Turkey.

**White man's burden** The perceived duty of white-ruled nations to govern so-called inferior races and countries.

Perhaps the most that could be hoped for, sooner or later, was that India would ↵ *Bengali elite hoped that* gain **Dominion status** within the Empire. Dominion status had been granted to Canada in 1867, Australia in 1901 and South Africa in 1910 (all of them white-ruled, of course). For India, the key question was whether India was yet a nation. Many certainly spoke of it as a nation in the making but many had doubts about ever unifying India under Indian rule.

## Nationalism

The late nineteenth century also saw the growing success of nationalist movements, based on recognition of peoples with their own shared history, language and culture and a right to self-determination. In some cases, the history was rather romanticised, if not completely false, and the future envisaged as dream rather than practicality. There were two complementary nationalist objectives: unification and **secession**. For example:

- In 1871 modern Germany was formed from the unification of hundreds of small independent states.
- In the same year, the regions of Italy fought free from the Austro-Hungarian Empire and unified as a nation-state.
- In Ireland, Britain's oldest colonial conquest, there was a growing and violent nationalist movement but a bill to provide home rule in Ireland was defeated in 1886.
- The British had defeated the Boers in South Africa in 1902 but soon granted political equality.
- Nationalist wars in the Balkans in the early years of the twentieth century would provide the trigger for the First World War.

Moreover, the outcome of the Russo-Japanese war of 1904–5 was a sign of a changing world order: a small Asian country had defeated a great European power. ↳ *One asian country could do it so could India*

### The growth of nationalism in India

It has been argued that the 1858 Royal Proclamation laid the foundation for the nationalist movement in India. By 1900 there was a growing sense of a nation in the making because of:

- a growth in public **secular** education and in intellectual and cultural debate
- modernising of religious attitudes among both Hindus and Muslims
- a gradual increase in education in the English language
- opening of jobs in the ICS to Indian applicants
- expansion of the railway network, permitting the circulation across the whole of India of English-language newspapers.

As a result, the growing Indian middle class became the fertile soil of the nationalist movement (see Source C on page 14).

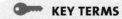

**KEY TERMS**

**Dominion status**
A category of self-government within the British Empire denoting a full nation.

**Secession** The formal breakaway of one part of a country.

**Secular** Public, non-religious affairs.

? What does Source C tell
  us about nationalist feeling
  in India at the beginning of
  the twentieth century?

### SOURCE C

**From an anonymous letter by an educated Muslim, quoted in Valentine Chirol,
*Indian Unrest*, Macmillan, 1910, p. 123.**

*English observers must not forget that there is throughout India amongst
Hindus a strong tendency towards imitating the national movements that have
proved successful in European history. Now, while* vis-à-vis *[with regard to]
the British, the Hindu irreconcilables assume the attitude of the Italian patriots
towards the hated Austrian,* vis-à-vis *the Moslems there is a very different
European model for them to follow. Not only Tilak [Bal Gangadhar Tilak, see
below] and his school in Poona but throughout the Punjab and Bengal the
constant talk of Nationalists is that the Moslems must be driven out of India as
they were driven out of Spain [after 1492].*

## Aligarh and the Muslim League

The Muslim community, anxious to throw off blame for the mutiny, took a
leading role in education and modernisation. In 1875 the Muslim Anglo-
Oriental College was founded at Aligarh. The college gave its name to a broad
movement across India with the aim of increasing Muslim prominence in social
affairs. The movement also initiated the idea of two self-respecting communities
within India (Hindu and Muslim). In 1913 the college became a full university.

The fury of Hindus over the creation of a Muslim-majority province in the
partition of Bengal had convinced Muslims that, as and when Indians were
permitted to take part in government, Muslims would be overwhelmed by the
general Hindu majority.

As a result, in December 1906 the All-India Muslim League was founded at
Dacca, Bengal. Although for many years it was little more than a debating society
for its educated, middle-class members, the Muslim League would eventually
become, under its final leader, **Muhammad Ali Jinnah**, the driving force for
partition and the creation of Muslim Pakistan (see his profile on page 69).

## Congress

The origin of the Indian National **Congress** lies in a meeting of educated
middle-class Indians at the Imperial **Durbar** of 1877. In 1885 it was constituted
as a political group and in due course became the driver of nationalist
independence campaigns. Both Hindus and Muslims came to Congress and
were prominent in its affairs. One early decision had been to ensure that its
discussions did not alienate religious groups and weaken its claim to speak for
all India.

Of course, there were no general elections in which it might put up candidates.
Congress adopted a strategy of lobbying MPs in Britain, so most of the early
Congress activity was directed at raising money to fund a small organisation
and newspaper in London. Most of the early demands of Congress related to
increasing education and access to positions in the administration of India.

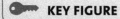

### KEY FIGURE

**Muhammad Ali Jinnah
(1875–1948)**

Leader of the Muslim League
and first governor-general of
Pakistan.

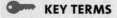

### KEY TERMS

**Congress** Originally a word
for a large meeting, later the
name of the political party
itself.

**Durbar** Imperial celebration.

In the early years of the twentieth century there was a split within Congress between moderates and radicals. The moderates, led by **Gopal Krishna Gokhale**, hoped for political reform and believed in peaceful, lawful methods. The radicals, led by **Bal Gangadhar Tilak**, argued that the lack of consultation over the Bengal partition showed that the British would never be fair to Indians. They wanted more urgent, direct, even violent action.

A later leader of Congress, **Mohandas Gandhi**, would become the national figurehead of the independence movement (see his profile on page 40).

## Changing British and Indian attitudes

During the late nineteenth century, the British elite became more aloof and racist. In the time of the East India Company, British merchants learned the local languages and even married local women. Now the deliberate growth of English language education meant there were many Indian translators. Raj society replicated upper-class society in the home country. The mutiny had left a long memory and complex attitudes among many of the British. They were distrustful and aware of how vulnerable they were as such a small minority protected by mainly Indian soldiers. Yet they could not help being contemptuous of Indian 'backwardness'.

### SOURCE D

**From memoranda by Viceroy Lord Ripon written in 1881–2, quoted in Judith Brown, *Modern India: The Origins of Asian Democracy*, Oxford University Press, 1994, pp. 106 and 133.**

*We cannot now rely on military force alone and policy as well as justice ought to prompt us to endeavour to govern more and more by means of and in accordance with that growing public opinion which is beginning to show itself throughout the country.*

*We shall not subvert the British Empire by allowing the Bengali baboo [**babu**] to discuss his own schools and drains. Rather shall we afford him a safety-valve if we can turn his attention to such innocuous subjects.*

### SOURCE E

**From a letter to the newspaper *Kesari* in 1900, quoted in S.R. Mehrotra, *Towards India's Freedom and Partition*, Vikas Publishing, 1978, p. 35.**

*We are thoroughly convinced that India cannot recover her national freedom in the real sense of the word independently of English protection, assistance and control. We are aware of the loss which we are at present suffering from British government yet we do not believe that our condition will be any better by the exchange of the British rule for that of any other nation … Since we are not in a position to gain our independence by fighting with the English or to preserve it when gained it is desirable that we should advance step by step behaving in a conciliatory manner with the British.*

 **KEY FIGURES**

**Gopal Krishna Gokhale (1866–1915)**

Leader of the moderate wing of Congress, opposed to violent protest.

**Bal Gangadhar Tilak (1856–1920)**

Leader of the radical wing of Congress, approved of violent protest, founder of the Home Rule League (1916).

**Mohandas Karamchand Gandhi (1869–1948)**

Later leader of the independence movement.

Compare and contrast Sources D and E for evidence of the attitudes of the British and Indians towards each other. **?**

 **KEY TERM**

**Babu** Bengali term for clerk.

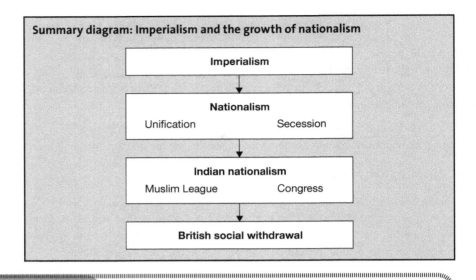

Summary diagram: Imperialism and the growth of nationalism

Imperialism

↓

Nationalism

Unification          Secession

↓

Indian nationalism

Muslim League          Congress

↓

British social withdrawal

## Chapter summary

This chapter has set out the historical development of the key social, cultural and political elements of India leading up to 1914. India was enormous and very diverse in all sorts of ways and had never been completely unified by any ruler or elite. At most, in the Mughal period and in the British Raj, hegemony had been extended over large parts of the subcontinent through treaties and paramountcy. The British were forced by the Indian Mutiny to recognise that if they wanted to retain power they had to exercise active control and engage with Indian political aspirations. At the same time, they attempted to deflect attention from the reality. Controlling an empire was expensive and like other imperialists they exploited the native population to pay for it. This was disguised by a moral obligation to educate and civilise the population and prepare them for self-government in the European style one day far in the future. As we shall see, their lack of commitment was disguised by exploitation of the disagreements between religious communities.

##  Refresher questions

Use these questions to remind yourself of the key material covered in this chapter.

1 What were the major communities in the Indian socio-political landscape?

2 What were the causes and consequences of the Indian Mutiny?

3 How did the princely states relate to the British Raj?

4 What were the reasons for the partition of Bengal?

5 How did the Indian Councils Act set a constitutional precedent for communities?

6 In what ways was India of strategic importance to the British Empire?

7 What were the origins of the Muslim League?

8 What were the origins of Congress?

9 How did British attitudes respond to a changing Indian society in the late nineteenth century?

10 What were the key elements of the system of British governance of India in the period up to 1914?

## CHAPTER 2

# The First World War and its impact on British India 1914–20

During the First World War India generally supported the British Empire but gained new perspectives on its values. There was moderate, and collaborative, nationalist agitation. Two future leaders began to make their name: Gandhi and Jinnah. Their relationship affects the rest of this history. Britain responded with a promise of constitutional progress but imposed harsh control measures, culminating in an atrocity which still tarnishes the British period. In the end, a major piece of constitutional legislation was regarded as too little, too late.

This chapter examines:

★ India and the First World War

★ War and the growth of nationalism

★ The effects of the war on British rule

## Key dates

| | | | |
|---|---|---|---|
| 1914 | Outbreak of the Great War (later called the First World War) | 1917 | Imperial War Conference |
| | | | Balfour Declaration |
| 1915 | Indian Army's Mesopotamian campaign | | Russian Revolution |
| | *Ghadr* agitation | 1918 | Armistice (end of war) |
| | Defence of India Act | 1919 | Rowlatt Act (Anarchical and Revolutionary Crimes Act) |
| 1916 | Formation of home rule leagues | | |
| Dec. | Lucknow Pact between Congress and Muslim League | April 13 | Amritsar Massacre |
| | | Dec. | Government of India Act 1919 (Montford Reforms) |
| 1917 Aug. | Montagu Declaration | | |

# India and the First World War

▶ *What was India's military involvement in the war?*

▶ *What impact did the war have on India's economy?*

Competition among the imperial powers turned into bloody conflict across Europe between 1914 and 1918. Thousands of Indians volunteered for military service, politicians pledged their loyalty and India made the largest contribution to the war effort from the British Empire. A total of 210,000 sepoys and 80,000 British Indian Army soldiers went overseas, leaving just 15,000 troops to maintain order in a country the size of Europe. The experience of war was to have a significant effect on the people and economy of India.

## The Indian response to war

Although not fighting to defend its homeland, it was apparent that the supreme global power of Britain was under threat. It was contesting with equally powerful forces and an easy victory was soon dismissed. Britain's alliance with Russia (and France) meant that a wartime threat to India from the north was inconceivable. However, in the event of Britain's defeat, then Russia might march in. This concentrated Indian minds on supporting the British war effort.

On the other hand, even in the event of victory, the war would be likely to have weakened Britain's power, creating much more favourable conditions for the nationalist movement.

It was, of course, not immediately obvious that the conflict would be a world war (nor indeed just the first). It involved nations with global empires but the predominant theatre of war was Europe, and the Western Front across Belgium and France in particular. Accordingly, Indian troops were transported to Europe to fight Germany (and the Austro-Hungarian Empire) and to the Middle East to attack the Ottoman Empire (ruled by the Turks), which had allied itself to Germany. The effect of the soldiers' experiences on Indian public opinion was significant.

## Indian military experiences and contribution

The moral high ground of the white man's burden turned into the blood-soaked swamp of trench warfare. To the Indians, the carnage of the Great War was proof that the Europeans were no better and perhaps worse than those they ruled. Indeed, the fighting between white European neighbours (and the family kinship of the German Kaiser, the Russian Tsar and the King-Emperor of Britain) could be described in the same terms as 'communal' fighting between Indian Hindus and Muslims.

European barbarity was aggravated by the incompetence of the major campaign involving Indian troops in **Mesopotamia** against the Turks in 1915. The British

 **KEY TERM**

**Mesopotamia** The Middle East, especially what is now Iraq, from the Greek for 'between rivers' (the Tigris and Euphrates in Iraq).

had been drawn into the Mesopotamian campaign by French and Russian desires to break up the Ottoman Empire. There was great British reluctance to go to war against this Islamic empire because of the possible reaction within India. However, it was strategically important to prevent the oil pipelines at Abadan (Persia), which supplied the Royal Navy, from falling to the Turks.

The troops were underequipped and badly led. Indian industry, underdeveloped in the imperialist system, could not at first produce weapons or vehicles and the British could not afford to divert supplies from the European war. The campaign, which was financed entirely by taxation on Indians, acquired the nickname the 'Mess-Pot'. Thirteen thousand Indian troops were **besieged** at Kut; 23,000 were killed trying to reach them. Forced to surrender, they were marched off across the desert to Turkey, most of them dying on the way.

## Economic impact

The war proved to be hugely costly both in terms of the enormous loss of life and financially. The British government paid for the war economy by borrowing $4 billion from the USA: the interest on this loan amounted to 40 per cent of government expenditure.

If the war had weakened the British imperial economy, it benefited Indian industry. According to historian Lawrence James, the Indian Tata Iron and Steel Company employed 7000 in 1907, but by 1923 this figure had risen to 30,000, enabling it to increase its output a hundredfold. This growth was largely driven by the need to supply Indian troops fighting in Mesopotamia with equipment and supplies.

There were other opportunities for India. Before the war, cotton, for example, had been farmed in India then shipped to Britain and the manufactured goods sold back to Indians. Economic historian Professor Alan Milward has described this as an example of the 'scaffolding of multilateral settlements, which before 1914 held together the structure of international trade'; in other words, a prime example of imperialist exploitation, resulting in a balance of payments deficit in India. The war diverted shipping from this trade, leading to a lack of cotton in Lancashire, unemployment and the near total collapse of the industry, while the Indian cotton industry was strengthened through finding new customers. By the end of the war, Japan and the USA bought as much Indian cotton as Britain did. In James's words: 'The war had fractured Anglo-Indian economic inter-dependency and started a trend that would become increasingly pronounced over the next twenty years.'

→ India also began to trade w/ other nations such as USA & Japan

These changes benefited owners as capitalists (sometimes referred to as war profiteering) but conditions were hard for workers and peasant farmers (*ryots*). Taxation nearly doubled to pay for the Mesopotamian campaign, including the equipment provided by Tata. The cost of food had also risen by 67 per cent by the end of the war. Towards the end of the war, industrial strikes increased

**KEY TERM**

**Besieged** Surrounded by the enemy but typically within a defensible fortification, creating a long stand-off.

dramatically (that is, strikes about wages and conditions rather than political agitation).

Finally, it is worth noting that economic activity was also weakened by the global **pandemic** of Spanish influenza in the winter of 1918–19, which killed more people than the war. India suffered more than any other country: 12.5 million (perhaps even 18 million) Indians died out of 21.5 million in the world as a whole.

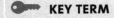

**KEY TERM**

**Pandemic** Global epidemic.

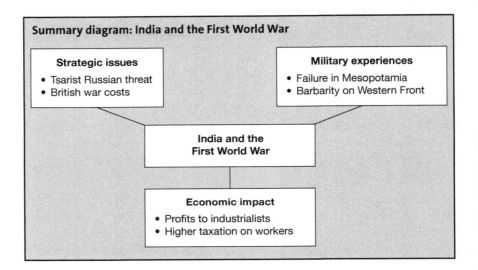

**Summary diagram: India and the First World War**

**Strategic issues**
- Tsarist Russian threat
- British war costs

**Military experiences**
- Failure in Mesopotamia
- Barbarity on Western Front

**India and the First World War**

**Economic impact**
- Profits to industrialists
- Higher taxation on workers

# 2 War and the growth of nationalism

▶ *How did the war affect Indian nationalist activity?*

Although Indian support for the war was strong, there were reminders that nationalist goals had not been forgotten by either extremists or moderates. The war period witnessed moderate, and collaborative, nationalist agitation and a number of important developments in the growth of Indian nationalism.

## The *Ghadr* movement

Most disturbing for the British were a number of mutinies. There were two early mutinies of Pathans in the winter of 1914–15, apparently caused by fear that they would be led by Muslim officers. Indian troops in Singapore had learned from reports and personal letters about the death toll at the Battle of the Somme (1916). A rumour that they were to embark for France led to a rampage and the killing of European civilians, including women. One woman wrote later of the incident that she thought the horrors of the 1857 mutiny were about to be repeated. In fact, order was quickly established and 37 ringleaders were publicly executed.

The most politically significant mutiny never actually took place. In early 1914 a Japanese steamer, the *Komagata Maru*, was commissioned by more than 300 Sikhs working in Malaya (present-day Malaysia) to take them to Canada. When the ship arrived in Vancouver, the Canadians refused entry despite the voyage complying with new anti-Asian immigration laws. After months in harbour, the *Komagata Maru* was forced to set sail for Calcutta.

By the time it arrived in India, in September 1914, war had broken out and suspicions were high. It was known that the Canadian coastal province of British Columbia was home to a growing movement of anti-British Indians. The movement gave its name – *Ghadr* – to a newspaper widely distributed in North America and the East, which had the subtitle 'enemy of the British government'.

> ### 🔑 KEY TERM
>
> *Ghadr* Translates as mutiny.

When the steamer docked, the Sikhs found troops waiting to escort them to a holding camp. Some made a break for the city and 22 were shot. The rest were rounded up and transported across India. The incident inflamed anti-British feeling in the Punjab, still more so when an official inquiry blamed the immigrant Sikhs.

Subsequently, British secret police paid close attention to politics in the Punjab. Inside information led to the break-up of a planned uprising in 1915. Five thousand Ghadrites were arrested, 200 were jailed or transported abroad and 46 were hanged. The relief and satisfaction of the British was haunted by the realisation that the traditional loyalty of the Punjab (compared with the continuous agitation of Bengal) could no longer be counted on. Just four years later, this anxiety would lead to the worst atrocity of British rule in India.

## Home rule leagues

### Origins

In 1916 two new political organisations were launched. Both had the aim of campaigning for home rule for India (and had almost identical names). One was led by the ejected Congress radical Tilak, the other by a forceful 69-year-old British woman called **Annie Besant**.

> ### 🔑 KEY FIGURE
>
> **Annie Besant (1847–1933)**
>
> Political and religious campaigner, founder of the All-India Home Rule League and president of Congress 1917–18.

The home rule leagues were based closely on the campaigns for home rule in Ireland in the late nineteenth century. An Irish parliamentary party had been formed to work democratically for self-government in Ireland while remaining part of the British Empire. It took four attempts between 1886 and 1914 for an Irish Home Rule Bill to become law and even then it was suspended because of the outbreak of war. There was a significant Irish uprising at Easter 1916.

In the Indian context, this struggle showed that home rule was a challenging but realistic objective. It could not be dismissed as too easy. Although Congress had discussed home rule since 1905, the control of the moderates had ensured that it never became a campaign. But Congress had lost momentum and influence since the 1907 split. Besant tried at first to work with Congress and revive its fortunes, but she soon realised that Congress was only interested in controlling and suppressing the home rule movement.

**SOURCE A**

From Mrs Besant's speech as president of Congress, December 1917, quoted in *The Thirty-Second Indian National Congress Calcutta*, Theosophical Publishing Society, 1917, pp. 22–34.

*India demands Home Rule for two reasons, one essential and vital, the other less important but weighty: First because Freedom is the birthright of every Nation: secondly, because her most important interests are now made subservient to the interests of the British Empire without her consent, and her resources are not utilised for her greatest needs. It is enough only to mention the money spent on her Army, not for local defence but for Imperial purposes, as compared with that spent on primary education.*

> ? In what ways do Besant's two contrasting arguments in Source A pose criticisms of the British?

## Home rule

Home rule was not revolutionary. Indeed, the term was adopted, in the opinion of one nationalist, N.C. Kelkar, because it was 'familiar to the English ear and saved them from all the imaginary terrors which the word *swaraj* was likely to conjure up in their minds'.

Home rule would only involve management of internal Indian affairs. Defence and foreign policy would remain matters for the British government. Besant stated that it meant 'freedom without separation'; Tilak emphasised that it sought 'reform of the system of administration and not the overthrow of government'. It was certainly not intended to harm the war effort. Tilak himself stated in 1917: 'If you want Home Rule be prepared to defend your Home … You cannot reasonably say that the ruling will be done by you and the fighting for you.'

> **KEY TERM**
>
> *Swaraj* Translates as self-rule.

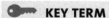

## Success

Tilak's Home Rule League for India rapidly gained 32,000 members despite being focused on just the two regions of Maharashtra and Karnataka. Besant's All-India Home Rule League was smaller and grew more slowly but its network of committees covered most of the rest of India. The two were mutually supportive: Tilak and Besant joined each other's organisations. They toured the country giving public lectures and publishing pamphlets. They successfully generated agitation among the public in a way that Congress had never really tried.

## Responses

Two future national leaders, Jinnah and **Jawaharlal Nehru**, joined the leagues but Gandhi refused, saying: 'Mrs Besant, you are distrustful of the British; I am not, and I will not help in any agitation against them during the war.'

> **KEY FIGURE**
>
> **Jawaharlal Nehru (1889–1964)**
>
> Up-and-coming nationalist figure, later Congress leader and prime minister of independent India.

Gandhi's view would soon change dramatically. Other Indian groups were also resistant, especially Muslims and lower-caste Hindu groups who thought that self-government would entrench Brahmin Hindu dominance. They viewed the British as more protective of their interests.

*[handwritten: were resistant]*

The British regarded the home rule leagues with great concern. They had finally calmed the agitation caused by the partition of Bengal by reuniting it in 1911 and liked the tame approach of the moderate-controlled Congress. One official reported: 'Moderate leaders can command no support among the vocal classes who are being led at the heels of Tilak and Besant.'

*[handwritten: → including Tilak & Besant]*

Orders were given for the swift arrest of home rule campaigners whenever possible. Students were forbidden from holding meetings at which home rule might be discussed. Tilak was arrested on charges of sedition and required to put up 40,000 **rupees** as **surety** of good behaviour. Besant was actually **interned**.

These moves were completely counter-productive. Congress moderates now swung their support over to home rule campaigns. The concerns of the new viceroy, Lord Chelmsford, are shown in Source B.

### KEY TERMS

**Rupee** The currency of India.

**Surety** A deposit lost in the event of breaking the law.

**Interned** Imprisoned without trial.

#### SOURCE B

**From a letter by the viceroy to the secretary of state, quoted in S.R. Mehrotra, *Towards India's Freedom and Partition*, Vikas Publishing, 1978, pp. 132–3.**

*Mrs Besant, Tilak and the others are fomenting with great vigour the agitation for immediate home rule and in the absence of any definite announcement by the government of India as to their policy in the matter, it is attracting many of those who hitherto have held less advanced views.*

What reason is given in Source B for increasing support for home rule movements?

## Consequences

When Besant was freed, she was triumphantly elected president of Congress in December 1917. There were great hopes for the reunification and revival of Congress. However, she proved an inconsistent and ineffective leader. Crucially, she was reluctant to support any kind of boycott or resistance campaign. Tilak still refrained from rejoining Congress.

*[handwritten: She was a bad leader]*

The home rule movement quickly lost momentum and, strictly speaking, it failed to achieve its objectives. However, it had created the first truly national mass campaign. Moreover, its failure left an unsatisfied willingness among the general population for more direct action. This is widely believed to have prepared the way for the campaigns of Gandhi from the 1920s onwards.

## The Lucknow Pact

The home rule agitation had somewhat bridged the distance between Congress and the Muslim League. At the Congress meeting of December 1916 in Lucknow, a historic agreement was reached, ending what Congress president A.C. Mazumdar described as 'ten years of painful separation … misunderstandings and the mazes of unpleasant controversies'.

In 1915 Congress and the Muslim League had held concurrent sessions in Bombay and both had declared self-government as their political objective. During 1916 two committees had worked together to prepare the details of a scheme for how such self-government would work. Concurrent sessions were again held in Lucknow which finalised the so-called Lucknow Pact, covering not only a broad statement of political objective but also the precise details of future electorates, once India was self-governing. The sense of occasion was further enhanced by the reintegration of the radical wing of the Congress Party at the same session. Although the scheme was accepted by the two political groups, it was not in their power to bring it about.

**Table 2.1** Muslim proportions of provincial populations and planned seats in provincial councils as part of the Lucknow Pact

| Province | Muslim population (%) | Planned seats (%) |
|---|---|---|
| Punjab | Over 50 | 50 |
| Bengal | Over 50 | 40 |
| United Provinces | 14 | 30 |
| Bihar | 13 | 25 |
| Central Provinces | 4 | 15 |
| Madras | 7 | 15 |
| Bombay | 20 | 33.3 |

The heart of the scheme was the setting of proportions of seats in the provincial legislative councils reserved for Muslims (see Table 2.1). This took forward the precedent created by the Indian Councils Act 1909 (see page 10) of separate communal elections for quotas of seats in the councils. What was remarkable was the extent to which Congress agreed to weighting the representation above the proportion of the actual population in many provinces.

Further communal agreements in the plan included:

*agreements made under Pact*

- No Muslim would contest a seat outside the reserved quota.
- No bill or clause would proceed if 75 per cent of the affected community opposed it.
- The central Legislative Council would increase to 150 members, of whom 80 per cent would be elected and one-third of them would be Muslim in the proportions set out for the provinces, thus giving Muslims additional weightage at both provincial and central levels.

There were more general agreements, such as:

- Councils would have powers over revenue collection, loans and expenditure.
- Indians would form at least half the members of the Executive Council.
- The judiciary would be independent of the executive, the government of India would be independent of the secretary of state, and the India Council in Britain would be abolished.
- Defence, foreign affairs and diplomacy would remain British responsibilities.

The Muslim League leader Jinnah stated that 'co-operation in the cause of the motherland should be our guiding principle'. To the British, it seemed that the nationalist movement was reuniting and gaining strength.

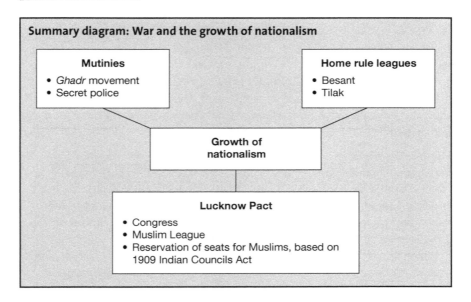

**Summary diagram: War and the growth of nationalism**

**Mutinies**
- *Ghadr* movement
- Secret police

**Home rule leagues**
- Besant
- Tilak

**Growth of nationalism**

**Lucknow Pact**
- Congress
- Muslim League
- Reservation of seats for Muslims, based on 1909 Indian Councils Act

# ③ The effects of the war on British rule

▶ *What impact did the war have on British rule?*

The end of the First World War could have been an opportunity for Britain to reward Indian loyalty and sacrifice. However, the British felt far from secure and could not stop themselves from extending wartime control. The resulting protest led to a massacre which was a turning point for the future of British control over India.

## Political consequences of the First World War

The First World War had a number of important political consequences which threatened British security. First, the Russian Revolution in 1917 had resulted in a **Bolshevik** government which had executed Tsar Nicholas II and his family. The Bolsheviks had also withdrawn from a war that they saw as a conflict between imperialists (and royal cousins). The European powers feared the spread of Bolshevism. British soldiers who had expected to return home in peacetime found themselves fighting inside Russia against a new Red Army in the vain hope of killing off the Bolshevik regime. Indian troops were deployed in the **North West Frontier Province** against Russian forces. In Britain, the police

 **KEY TERMS**

**Bolshevik** The group that emerged as leaders of the Russian Revolution.

**North West Frontier Province** One of the eleven British provinces of the Raj, adjoining Afghanistan and close to Russia (across the Hindu Kush mountains).

*[handwritten note: Spy branch was est. in the future would...]*

formed a Special Branch to spy and report on suspicious political activity. In due course, Special Branch officers in Britain and India would be reporting on Indian independence campaigners.

Second, potential defeat, as German troops from the Russian Front reinforced the Western Front, was averted only by the entry of the USA into the war. This foreshadowed the eclipse of the British Empire by the Americans during the twentieth century. President Woodrow Wilson felt sufficiently supreme to declare his so-called **Fourteen Points** of international policy. These included the right of peoples to independent nationhood. The constant US pressure to apply this principle to the British Empire would have major significance for the British in India.

> **KEY TERM**
>
> **Fourteen Points** US President Wilson's post-war principles of international policy.

*[handwritten note: US took charge in Post-war efforts]*

Third, it was hoped in India, among both British and Indian populations, that the Mesopotamian region would become a British-controlled buffer zone to protect the western approach to India. However, further political factors came into play. Irregular Arab forces (some led by Lawrence of Arabia) had scored minor, but spectacular, successes against Ottoman Turkish forces and supply lines. The British had promised them some form of independence once the Ottoman Empire was broken up. One such consequence was the creation of the Arab state of Iraq. The British in India were dismayed by this whole-hearted support for nationalist demands. How could similar demands within India be denied?

This was compounded by the Balfour Declaration of November 1917. Arthur Balfour, British foreign secretary, gave a contradictory guarantee that: (a) the British would assist in the creation of a homeland for the Jewish people in Palestine but also (b) the political rights of the existing Arab, mainly Muslim, peoples would not be threatened. This was recognition of a claim by a religious community to be a nation, entitled to its own state. Although Israel did not come into existence until 1948, the political precedent for the Indian, specifically Pakistani, situation would be uncomfortable.

## The Montagu Declaration

The British government realised the need to respond to both the Indian war effort and the new nationalist unity. India was permitted its own representatives at the Imperial War Conference of 1917. This gave it a status comparable to the self-governing Dominions of the British Empire. The conference was called to discuss the shape of the eventual political settlement after the expected victory of the Allied powers. When victory was finally achieved, India also took part in the formal peace treaty negotiations.

By 1917 it was also clear to the British that if it wanted to postpone actual political concessions until after the war, it needed to make a statement to counter the home rule movement and the Lucknow Pact. Accordingly, Edwin Montagu, secretary of state for India, announced a new constitutional objective in the House of Commons on 20 August (see Source C).

*Montague Declaration.*

## SOURCE C

**From the statement by Lord Montagu, secretary of state for India, to the House of Commons, 20 August 1917. Quoted in V.P. Menon, *Transfer of Power in India*, Orient Longman, 1957, p. 16.**

*The Policy of His Majesty's Government, with which the Government of India are [sic] in complete accord, is that of the increasing association of Indians in every branch of the administration and the gradual development of self-governing institutions with a view to the progressive realisation of responsible government in India as part of the British Empire. They have decided that substantial steps in this direction should be taken as soon as possible, and that it is of the highest importance as a preliminary to considering what these steps should be that there should be free and informal exchange of opinion between those in authority at home and in India.*

> What does Source C reveal about the commitment of the British government?

Montagu promptly set off on a massive tour of India to consult politicians and public opinion. His findings were published in the 1918 Montagu–Chelmsford Report, which would become the basis for the 1919 legislation. However, by the time the reforms became law, events at Amritsar in the Punjab would have sealed the fate of the British Empire in India.

## The Rowlatt Act

In this insecure state of affairs the British were not inclined to relax their guard in India, despite or perhaps because of the commitment given in the Montagu Declaration. The British government in India had passed the Defence of India Act (1915), permitting them to close down newspapers suspected of anti-British attitudes for the duration of the war. Comparing it with the **Defence of the Realm Act** in Britain, Viceroy Lord Hardinge later boasted that it was 'a far more drastic Dora than her English sister'.

*overkill*

Indians had expected that with the end of the war these measures would become inactive, if not explicitly repealed. In fact, the British quickly moved to renew their powers by passing the Anarchical and Revolutionary Crimes Act (1919), now more commonly termed the Rowlatt Act, after its creator.

The Act enabled the powers of the Defence of India Act to be invoked if it was judged that **anarchic** conditions were developing. These powers included unlimited detention without trial, trial without jury and the use of evidence illegal in peacetime. A wide range of activities constituted anarchic behaviour. For example, it was now an offence punishable by two years' imprisonment to possess a copy of a **seditious** newspaper.

All 22 Indian members of the Imperial Legislative Council had opposed the bill but the majority, consisting of appointed officials, ensured that it was passed.

The 1919 Hunter Inquiry (see page 30) identified the Rowlatt Act as the most significant grievance of Indians (see Source D).

**KEY TERMS**

**Defence of the Realm Act** British emergency law passed four days after the declaration of war, creating censorship and prohibiting certain activities (including all-day pub opening hours).

**Anarchic** Without structure, tending towards political chaos.

**Seditious** Encouraging overthrow of a government.

Using Sources D and E, how would you describe the attitudes to the Act of the Indian people and the Indian members of the Legislative Council? Do you detect a difference of British attitude in the sources?

## SOURCE D

**From the report of the committee appointed to investigate disturbances in the Punjab (set up by the British Parliament and chaired by Lord Hunter, commonly referred to as the Hunter Inquiry). Quoted in William Hunter, *Report of Committee Appointed to Investigate the Disturbances in the Punjab*, Cmd 681, HMSO, 1920, pp. 29–31.**

*The opposition to the Rowlatt Bills [sic] was very widespread throughout India among both moderate and extreme politicians. It was represented that, on the eve of the grant of a large measure of self-government to India [following the Montagu Declaration], and after the splendid contribution made by her to the winning of the European war, there was no necessity for passing an Act of the character proposed. It was objected that the Act conferred considerable power on the Executive uncontrolled by the Judiciary. It was maintained that the Defence of India Act clothed the Government with all the authority they would get under the new legislation [the Rowlatt Act], and that there was, therefore, every reason for delay and for conceding an adjournment asked by the Indian members of the Legislative Council. The agitation against Government action took an acute form in the months of February and March, both in the press and on public platforms.*

However, Viceroy Lord Chelmsford wrote about the Indian members of the Legislative Council (see Source E).

## SOURCE E

**From a letter to the King-Emperor, 21 May 1919, quoted in P.N. Chopra, Prabha Chopra and Padmsha Jha, *Secret Papers from British Royal Archives*, Konark Publishing, 1998, p. 193.**

*It was impossible for my Government to ignore [the Rowlatt Commission reporting on extension of the Defence of India Act after the end of the war] and consequently we felt it incumbent upon us to introduce legislation strictly following their recommendations. This legislation was introduced in the February Session of this year in my Legislative Council, and it was immediately evident that we should have the unanimous opposition of all the non-official Indian Members. I must say that the opposition, while unanimous on the surface, was by no means unanimous in reality, for many of the non-official Indian Members expressed privately their conviction that the legislation was necessary but they felt unable to resist the pressure put upon them to oppose these Bills. We felt however that we must face this opposition and that we could not take the grave responsibility of ignoring the weighty recommendations ... and consequently we put the legislation through by means of our official majority. It was clear that the extremist party in India was determined to make what use it could of this legislation as a peg on which to hang a widespread agitation against Government throughout India.*

Jinnah resigned from the Council, stating that the Act 'ruthlessly trampled upon the principles for which Great Britain avowedly fought the war'.

Gandhi declared it a betrayal of wartime support by Indians and declared a national **hartal** on 6 April 1919, which was widely supported and reinforced the alarming unity of Hindu and Muslim campaigners. The *hartal* turned to widespread violence, not least in the cities of the Punjab, unleashing the terrible events at Amritsar in 1919.

The Bengali poet Rabindranath Tagore would later describe the Amritsar Massacre as 'the monstrous progeny of a monstrous war'.

**SOURCE F**

**An unknown artist's impression of the aftermath of the Amritsar Massacre, April 1919.**

> 🔑 **KEY TERM**
>
> **Hartal** Translates as strike action, refusal to work.

> How does Source F represent the scale of the Amritsar Massacre? **?**

## The Amritsar Massacre

Amritsar is the holy city of the Sikhs at the centre of the Punjab. Punjabis had played a major role in the war, but also in the *Ghadr* movement. There was a strong mood of resentment at the continued repression in the form of the Rowlatt Act. On the British side, there was a renewed fear of uprising and mutiny.

### The Jallianwala Bagh meeting

Congress declared another *hartal* for 8 April 1919, which was widely supported but led to violent attacks on people and buildings. On 10 April a mob killed five Englishmen and left an Englishwoman for dead. The Punjab provincial government requested military assistance and control.

Troops under the command of General Dyer arrived in Amritsar on the evening of 11 April. Dyer banned all public meetings and arrested local politicians. Dyer was determined not to repeat the accepted error of the 1857 mutiny by letting events get out of control. As he explained later, he was even more determined to teach the Punjabis a lesson.

Dyer's ban was defied by a public meeting on 13 April in the Jallianwala Bagh. This was an open space within the town that had originally been a set of gardens, but was now enclosed on all sides by the backs of buildings and a high wall. Between 10,000 and 20,000 Punjabis were crammed into the garden when Dyer arrived with Indian troops. He also had an armoured car with a machine gun on top. It is a small mercy that this was unable to enter the garden because the alleyway was too small.

Dyer's troops ran in, took up line position and, without warning, started firing into the crowd. There were only three or four other, very narrow, exits. Panic ensued and people were crushed together. Dyer interpreted this as the gathering of a charge and directed fire into the thickest groups. His troops used over 1600 bullets and only stopped firing because the ammunition ran out. Dyer later confirmed that had there been more ammunition he would have continued the onslaught. It is accepted that 379 people were killed within minutes. The 1200 wounded were left to fend for themselves.

In the days that followed, Dyer imposed **martial law** and humiliating punishments. Public floggings were held of Indians suspected, but not convicted, of violence. In the street where an Englishwoman had been attacked, Indians were forced to crawl along the ground.

### The Hunter Inquiry

British and worldwide concern eventually forced the government to hold an inquiry, chaired by Lord Hunter. In various statements to the Hunter Inquiry committee and elsewhere, Dyer made it abundantly clear that: 'It was no longer a question of merely dispersing the crowd but one of producing a sufficient moral effect, from a military point of view, not only on those who were present, but more especially throughout the Panjab. There could be no question of undue severity.'

Dyer maintained that the situation was on the verge of complete mob challenge to the British authority in India and a threat to the lives of Europeans. In this view, he was clearly supported by British public opinion, to the lasting disgust of Indians. The House of Lords passed a vote of thanks for Dyer's actions and a public subscription raised thousands of pounds in reward. By contrast, Rabindranath Tagore repudiated his own knighthood.

The inquiry report identified that the Rowlatt Act was 'largely, if not mainly, responsible for creating the feeling against the Government which promoted such serious disorder in the Punjab' but listed the following additional causes of the incident:

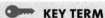
additonal causes

- arrest of Gandhi and general unrest
- home rule activity
- restrictions resulting from the Defence of India Act
- press criticism

> **KEY TERM**
>
> **Martial law** Military government, where the army imposes its own rules and suspends civil courts and justice.

- false rumours
- passive resistance
- *satyagraha*
- peace terms with Turkey
- high prices.

It specifically ruled out conspiracy.

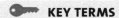

> **KEY TERMS**
>
> **Satyagraha** Translates as truth-force, a term coined by Gandhi to describe non-violent protest.
>
> **Censure** A formal political reprimand.

The inquiry committee was split along ethnic lines. The majority report held Dyer responsible but only **censured** him. The minority report of the three Indian members of the inquiry blamed martial law for the agitation and compared Dyer's actions to the brutality of the Germans during the war.

Even to the majority, it was inexcusable that Dyer did not attempt to prevent the meeting coming together and that he agreed that he could have dispersed the crowd without firing but would have 'looked a fool'.

Dyer's weak excuses, on top of his declared aim of terrorising the entire Punjab, have led some nationalist writers to claim that the massacre was planned. There is no evidence of this but in any case it was certainly a terrible misjudgement because the moral authority of the British was forever broken. Never again could the British claim to be ruling India with the aim of developing civilised public values or even that they governed by the rule of law.

The inquiry report concluded rather drily: 'The employment of excessive measures is likely as not to produce the opposite result to that desired.' Gandhi declared more forcefully: 'co-operation in any shape or form with this satanic government is sinful'. The freedom struggle was reinvigorated. In the view of historian Percival Spear, Dyer believed his actions were saving the Empire but Amritsar spelled the end of the Raj.

## Government of India Act 1919

The Montagu–Chelmsford Report of 1918 led to the Government of India Act 1919, more commonly known as the Montagu–Chelmsford Reforms (or even Mont–Ford Reforms). The provisions of the Act were implemented in 1921.

In the British view, this showed that the government was clearly following through the promise of the 1917 Montagu Declaration. To Indians, however, the four years from declaration to implementation contrasted significantly with the weeks taken to pass the repressive Rowlatt Act. Moreover, coming just eight months after the Amritsar Massacre, there was little feeling of success, let alone gratitude.

The Act contained three significant features:

- self-government in the future
- changes to the composition of councils and the electorate
- division of governmental responsibilities.

**SOURCE G**

? How does Source G characterise British authority?

'Progress to Liberty – Amritsar style.' A newspaper cartoon by David Low published in *The Star*, 16 December 1919.

## Self-government

The Act confirmed the promise of eventual self-government of India by an Indian Parliament. It promised a review in ten years' time of the success of the actual changes in the Act. Then a decision about the next move to Dominion status might be taken. It made no reference to independence from Britain at any time.

## Councils and electorates

The most significant feature in this area was the elimination of the majorities of appointed officials in most legislative councils. For the first time, members elected by Indians would be in the majority.

At the very top, the Imperial Executive Council was increased to six members, of whom three would be (appointed) Indians, plus the viceroy and the commander-in-chief.

The two houses of the central legislature comprised the (lower) Legislative Assembly, in which 106 members would be elected and 40 nominated, and the (higher) Council of State, which would have 61 members (elected by the wealthiest individuals).

The provincial Legislative Councils were expanded so that 70 per cent of members were elected. All provinces now had full governors and executive councils.

With regard to the electorate, the national **franchise** was extended according to levels of property tax, in other words, to wealthy males. Out of a population of some 150 million people, 5 million were able to vote for provincial councils, 1 million for the Legislative Assembly and just 17,000 for the Council of State.

Furthermore, the principle of separate candidates and electorates was firmly embedded. As well as general electorates, in which all those enfranchised could vote, there were 'reserved' elections of Muslim, Sikh and Christian members by their own electorates (subject still to the property qualification). There were also special electorates for universities (as in Britain until 1950), landholders and business interests.

**KEY TERM**

**Franchise** The conditions making people eligible to vote.

### SOURCE H

**From *The Report on Indian Constitutional Reforms*, Cmd 9109, HMSO, 1918, pp. 229–31.**

*Division by creeds and classes means the creation of political camps organised against each other, and teaches men to think as partisans and not as citizens; and it is difficult to see how the change from this system to national representation is ever to occur. The British Government is often accused of dividing men in order to govern them. But if it unnecessarily divides them at the very moment when it professes to start them on the road to governing themselves, it will find it difficult to meet the charge of being hypocritical or short-sighted.*

*A minority which is given special representation owing to its weak and backward state, is positively encouraged to settle down into a feeling of satisfied security;*

*We regard any system of communal electorates, therefore, as a very serious hindrance to the development of the self-governing principle … At the same time we must face the hard facts. The Muhammadans [Muslims] were given special representation with separate electorates in 1909 [Indian Councils Act] … Much as we regret the necessity, we are convinced that so far as the Muhammadans at all events are concerned the present system must be maintained until conditions alter, even at the price of slower progress towards the realisation of a common citizenship.*

Study Source H. How does the argument shift across this sequence of paragraphs? How might different Indian nationalist groups feel about the final position?

## Dyarchy

The new division of responsibilities at two levels within the administration of India was termed **dyarchy**. In the first place, responsibility for a number of matters was transferred from the central Indian government to provincial administrations. The provinces became responsible for collecting land tax, **excise** duty and revenue from stamps. The provinces were made responsible for their irrigation works. The central government retained responsibility for income tax, customs duties, salt tax, postal communications and railways, as well as defence and foreign affairs. This division was regarded as a pragmatic delegation rather than a concession of potential **federal** organisation.

At the level of provincial administration, there was perhaps an even more significant division. Matters were deemed to be either 'reserved' or 'transferred'. Reserved matters – characterised as law, order and revenue – would remain the responsibility of the governor's executive council. Transferred matters – characterised as developmental and nation-building – would become the responsibility of the elected legislative council to which provincial ministers would be accountable. For the first time, Indian politicians would hold ministerial power subject to oversight by predominantly Indian councils (see Figure 2.1).

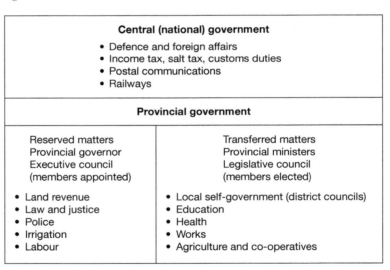

| Central (national) government |
|---|
| • Defence and foreign affairs |
| • Income tax, salt tax, customs duties |
| • Postal communications |
| • Railways |

| Provincial government | |
|---|---|
| Reserved matters<br>Provincial governor<br>Executive council<br>(members appointed) | Transferred matters<br>Provincial ministers<br>Legislative council<br>(members elected) |
| • Land revenue<br>• Law and justice<br>• Police<br>• Irrigation<br>• Labour | • Local self-government (district councils)<br>• Education<br>• Health<br>• Works<br>• Agriculture and co-operatives |

**Figure 2.1** Dyarchic government.

## Reactions

With hindsight, 1919 saw the temporary end of anarchic terrorist attacks and the end of military repression. However, it also marked the end of hope for moderate, gradual constitutional change.

Indian nationalist reaction to the 1919 Act was lukewarm. The provisions of the Act were complex and confusing. In fact, an inquiry would be launched in 1924–5 to review the breakdown of the political system created. The Act did not seem worth the prolonged wait during which expectations had built up. There was no point in not taking up the opportunities offered by the Act but there was a readiness to demand much more. The nationalist movement was about to be transformed from a small political elite pressing for concessions to a genuinely mass protest movement with demands for complete independence.

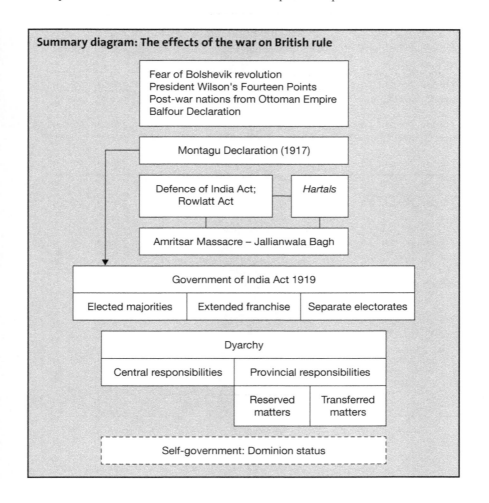

**Summary diagram: The effects of the war on British rule**

Fear of Bolshevik revolution
President Wilson's Fourteen Points
Post-war nations from Ottoman Empire
Balfour Declaration

Montagu Declaration (1917)

Defence of India Act; Rowlatt Act — *Hartals*

Amritsar Massacre – Jallianwala Bagh

Government of India Act 1919

| Elected majorities | Extended franchise | Separate electorates |

Dyarchy

| Central responsibilities | Provincial responsibilities |

Reserved matters — Transferred matters

Self-government: Dominion status

# Chapter summary

In this chapter we have seen that, although victorious in the war, Britain was damaged economically and reputationally. The civilised values of the European imperial powers were soaked in the blood of the conflict and the Amritsar Massacre. The war destroyed the Russian, Ottoman and Austro-Hungarian Empires, from which modern nation-states were created. The new global power appeared to be the USA, itself a former colony of Britain and a champion of national self-determination.

Britain declined to commit to eventual self-government for India, even though it had granted home rule to Ireland, assisted in Arab independence and promised Jews their own homeland. It continued to maintain repressive control over Indian politics by criminalising many activities. At Amritsar, a combination of panic and imperial arrogance led to an atrocity which still tarnishes the British Raj.

By the time Britain passed the Government of India Act, Indian nationalist opinion had moved on, partly through disgust with, and distrust of, the British and partly through an awakening sense of a new international order. The age of empires was coming to an end.

 Refresher questions

Use these questions to remind yourself of the key material covered in this chapter.

1 How did the conduct of the First World War change Indian views of British (European) superiority?

2 What were the political and economic consequences of the war for Britain and India?

3 What evidence was there of military unrest among Indian troops?

4 What were the objectives and outcomes of the home rule leagues?

5 Why was the Lucknow Pact significant?

6 What did the Montagu Declaration promise?

7 Why did the Rowlatt Act stir up trouble?

8 Contrast the Indian and British reactions to the Amritsar Massacre.

9 What new features were introduced in the Government of India Act 1919?

10 Explain in your own words the term dyarchy.

Question practice

## ESSAY QUESTIONS

1  How accurate is it to say that the Indian home rule leagues, in the years 1916–19, were largely successful?

2  To what extent did the First World War weaken the British imperial grip on India?

3  How far do you agree that the Amritsar Massacre of 1919 was the turning point in Britain's relationship with its empire in India, in the years 1914–45?

4  'The constitutional reforms brought in by the Government of India Act 1919 failed to satisfy the demands of Indian nationalists.' How far do you agree with this statement?

## SOURCE ANALYSIS QUESTIONS

1  Why is Source H (page 33) valuable to the historian for an enquiry into the British government's thoughts, on the difficulties of Indian constitutional reform, in the years 1909–19? Explain your answer using the source, the information given about it and your own knowledge of the historical context.

2  How much weight do you give the evidence of Source H (page 33) for an enquiry into British attitudes towards the Indian citizenry during the First World War? Explain your answer using the source, the information given about it and your own knowledge of the historical context.

3  How far could the historian make use of Sources D and E (page 28) together to investigate the causes of the Amritsar Massacre in 1919? Explain your answer using both sources, the information given about them and your own knowledge of the historical context.

## CHAPTER 3

# Changing political relationships 1920–30

The post-war period is stamped with the personality of Mahatma Gandhi. He brought a new style to Indian nationalism involving the mass of the people rather than an educated elite. He adopted the tactics of peaceful protest and added a spiritual dimension which the British found difficult to deal with. Imprisonment was no longer a deterrent. Jinnah and the Muslim League were in the shadow of Congress, sometimes finding common cause, sometimes insisting on differences.

This chapter examines:

★ Gandhi and civil disobedience

★ The British response: control and concession

★ Congress and the Muslim League

The key debate on *page 54* of this chapter asks the question: How does the portrayal of the nationalist leaders by historians influence judgements about the ultimate success or failure of the independence campaign?

## Key dates

| | | | | | |
|---|---|---|---|---|---|
| 1919–21 | | Non-cooperation campaigns | 1928 | | Simon Commission in India |
| 1922 | Feb. 6 | End of non-cooperation | | Aug. | Nehru Report presented at all-parties conference |
| | March 10 | Arrest of Gandhi | 1929 | March | Jinnah's Fourteen Points |
| 1924 | | Abolition of the Ottoman Khilafat | | Oct. | Dominion Declaration by British government |
| | | Release of Gandhi | | Dec. | Congress declared *purna swaraj* as objective |
| 1927 | | Delhi resolution of Muslim League | | | |

 # Gandhi and civil disobedience

▶ *How did Gandhi mobilise widespread political protest?*

Mahatma (Great Soul) Gandhi was one of the great figures of the twentieth century and will be forever associated with the concepts of non-violent protest and civil disobedience. He was not the first to develop or practise this approach but his various campaigns drew international attention because of the complex problems they caused the British. They were often unsuccessful in their precise objectives but there is agreement that, overall, Gandhi's genius was to recognise that the British Empire could be defeated by mass, peaceful, passive confrontation. His campaigns exposed the fact the Empire survived because of Indian support and that if that was withdrawn, it could not continue.

## Gandhi's aims and beliefs

Gandhi was propelled to national stature by the reaction to the Rowlatt Act and the Amritsar Massacre and by capturing popular imagination through his style of campaigning for Indian independence. Before then Gandhi was a promising but no longer youthful politician in the Congress Party, which itself remained a middle-class organisation for proposing constitutional change. Gandhi dominated Congress from 1920 until his death, although he was only formally president in 1924. Gandhi wanted to rid India of the British Raj and replace it with *swaraj* (self-rule). His vision, however, was not of a modern state but an imagined return to an almost medieval, highly religious society and peasant economy.

Gandhi perceived life as an integrated struggle for social justice and self-control. One controversial aspect of his self-control was sexual. For example, from 1906, he abstained from sexual intercourse with his wife, Kasturba, for the rest of their married life (she died in 1944) in order to preserve his energy and focus for *satyagraha*. However, his entourage included numerous young Indian and foreign women. To test and prove his powers of self-control, Gandhi insisted on sleeping naked between two such followers, despite the strong criticisms of Congress leaders.

Gandhi's methods were a powerful combination of spiritual strength, political skill and sheer theatricality. His campaigning was guided by four key principles:

### Satyagraha

*Satyagraha* is the root concept which Gandhi developed through his legal campaigning work for Indians in South Africa. He described it as 'not predominantly civil disobedience but a quiet and irresistible pursuit of truth'.

*Satyagraha* requires the rejection of dishonourable motives such as campaigning for the advantage of one religious community over another. It also involves a willingness to suffer for the cause, either by placing oneself in the path of physical violence or by engaging voluntarily in painful symbolic actions such as hunger strikes.

### Ahimsa

*Ahimsa* is a practical and political method developed out of *satyagraha*. In a political campaign for independence, peace and justice, it is unacceptable to use

**KEY TERM**

**Ahimsa** Literal meaning is non-violence.

# Mohandas Karamchand Gandhi

| | |
|---|---|
| 1869 | Born in Porbander, western India |
| 1888 | Became a law student in London |
| 1893 | Practised as a lawyer in South Africa |
| 1915 | Returned to India |
| | Started to be referred to as Mahatma ('Great Soul') Gandhi |
| 1919–21 | Non-cooperation movement |
| 1930 | Salt March and civil disobedience campaign |
| 1932 | Civil disobedience campaign |
| 1942 | Quit India movement |
| 1948 | Assassinated |

Gandhi was born, the youngest of six, into the Bania caste in the Gujarat region. Banias are typically grocers and the term is sometimes used to imply a selfish bargainer. In fact, his father was chief minister at the court of an Indian prince. Gandhi was married in 1882 to Kasturba and later had four sons. From his days as a law student in London, he lived frugally and on a strict vegetarian diet.

After being thrown off a train for being Indian in South Africa, he committed himself to work against racial discrimination. In 1906 he committed his first act of *satyagraha*: refusing to register under the racial pass laws.

Gandhi returned to India in January 1915 with a considerable reputation. He was at first motivated by a desire for Hindu–Muslim friendship and unity. He also campaigned ceaselessly for the social inclusion of the so-called Untouchables. However, he could be naïvely condescending and came close to stating that Muslims would eventually become Hindus. He was frequently contradictory and inconsistent in both statements and political tactics. Over time, his political objectives gradually became more inflexible. Most commentators agree that his rejection of Western values and of the entire concept of progress was actually counter-productive in the final stages of the independence movement.

Gandhi's ripostes could be withering. Dressed only in his shawl and loincloth, he met King George V at Buckingham Palace in London. When Gandhi was asked by newspaper reporters if he had been appropriately dressed, he responded that the King-Emperor had been wearing enough for both of them. Famously, when asked what he thought of Western civilisation, Gandhi replied that he thought it would be a good thing.

During the Second World War Gandhi called on the British to 'Quit India', wrote amicably to Hitler and recommended passive resistance to the British people. However, his immense personal bravery was demonstrated when he lived in Muslim areas to halt massacres at the time of partition. His support for Muslims led to his assassination by a Hindu extremist in 1948.

provocative or retaliatory violence. Accordingly, the campaign methods used involve inaction, withdrawal of co-operation, resignations, *hartals* (see page 29), boycotts or even just silence. In the face of physical force, campaigners must submit with dignity, relying on the moral effect of their suffering to provoke guilt in the attacker and a crisis of conscience and determination.

### Swadesh

*Swadesh* pre-dates Gandhi's political prominence. *Swadesh* emerged as a response to the 1905 partition of Bengal in a commitment to abstain from the purchase of British goods (see page 10). It is entirely Gandhian in its dignified avoidance of a particular action, even at personal cost or discomfort. Gandhi, however, took it further. He urged supporters, and required his close followers, to learn how to spin cloth and to spend an hour a day spinning in order to increase personal and national economic self-reliance. Clothes made of home-spun cloth, **khadi**, became a sign of political commitment, especially at high-level negotiations. From 1921 Gandhi himself chose to wear the peasant **dhoti**.

### Swaraj

Gandhi had written a book while in South Africa entitled *Hind Swaraj* (*Indian Self-rule*). He would declare *swaraj* as a political goal in his first campaigns and the Swaraj Party was formed in 1923.

## The non-cooperation campaign

Gandhi's first actions in India were in two industrial disputes in Bihar and in Gujarat in 1917. The Bihar campaign on behalf of workers growing indigo (for dyeing cloth) was a notable success. Gandhi interviewed workers and compiled a report, detailing the way landowners were exploiting their weakness in competition against synthetic dyes, which forced the authorities to intervene in their support. Gandhi was seen as a man of results for ordinary people rather than just a political speaker.

In 1919 Gandhi gained a narrow majority in Congress for a national campaign of protest about the Rowlatt Act and the Amritsar Massacre (see pages 27–31). The movement swelled into a loosely organised protest movement largely consisting of *hartals*, supported by both Hindus and Muslims, which alarmed the British. Gandhi, however, in a pattern that was to repeat itself, suspended the campaign when it turned violent.

At the Nagpur meeting of Congress, held in December 1920, Gandhi's proposal for an even larger non-cooperation movement was unanimously approved. Disgust at British popular support for General Dyer, perpetrator of the Amritsar Massacre, turned into support for Gandhi's call for 'a peaceful rebellion'. Gandhi declared the aim of *swaraj* within one year, a barely realistic objective but one which touched the mass of Indian population which had hitherto left politics to a middle-class elite.

The protest campaigns included boycotts of law courts by lawyers, of schools and colleges by teachers, and in general of elections, councils, official functions and honours. *Swadesh* was promoted and alcohol prohibited within the movement. A boycott of British cloth had an economic effect on British manufacturers. Boycotts became huge demonstrations during the visit to India by the Prince of Wales in 1921. Thirty thousand people were arrested. Agitation was rising across the whole country.

It was now apparent that Gandhi was not only the successor to the departed leaders of Congress, Gokhale and Tilak, but also able to create mass support through imagination and symbolism. Even more importantly, he opened up a new kind of politics between the failed approaches of pleading for constitutional

**KEY TERMS**

**Khadi** Home-spun cloth or clothing.

**Dhoti** Loin cloth.

concessions and counter-productive terrorist attacks. Gandhi's methods were non-violent but assertive. They did not rely on the humiliating notion of proving that educated Indians were becoming able to govern. They gave the masses a part to play with pride.

As the disturbances grew, some Indian leaders, including Jinnah, tried to get the viceroy to find a political way forward. He was sympathetic to the idea and proposed a **round table conference**. Gandhi, however, demanded the release of all prisoners jailed during the protests, including Khilafatists. The viceroy refused and the plan fell through.

### Khilafat

Gandhi also lent his support to the Indian *Khilafat*, part of an international Muslim movement of protest against the post-war break-up of the Ottoman (Turkish) Empire by the British and French. Gandhi spoke at national *Khilafat* meetings and urged Muslim non-cooperation with the British Raj.

The position of the Turkish **Sultan** was precarious and this was perceived as an attack on the international Muslim community. In India, Muslim opinion had turned against the British, not least because it was the British who had removed the last Mughal emperor in 1858, after the Indian Mutiny. In 1920 Congress passed a resolution in support of *Khilafat*. Even the viceroy, Lord Reading, had argued with the British government over the issue.

The *Khilafat* movement combined with the general Indian non-cooperation movement to create a powerful sense of anti-British Hindu–Muslim unity. It would not last, however.

## The end of non-cooperation

At the Ahmedabad session of Congress in December 1921, it was agreed to launch a mass civil disobedience campaign unless the issues of the *Khilafat* and the Amritsar Massacre were redressed. As this third campaign got under way, Gandhi suddenly called it off as a result of growing communal violence.

### The Moplah rebellion

A rebellion had already broken out, early in 1921, in the Malabar region, largely populated by the Moplahs, descendants of the earliest Muslim Arab traders. Agitation caused by the non-cooperation movement and the *Khilafat* was exacerbated by resentment against rich local landlords. A small altercation led to police reinforcements, further resentment and rioting.

At this point, the Moplahs turned on their Hindu neighbours. Over 600 were killed and 2500 forcibly converted to Islam. The provincial government called in troops and martial law was ruthlessly imposed in a prolonged rerun of the Amritsar situation. Over 2000 rebels were killed, including 66 left to suffocate in a train wagon. The ominous character of the communal violence cast a shadow over the non-cooperation and nationalist movement.

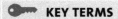
**KEY TERMS**

**Round table conference** A meeting of all parties with all opinions equally considered.

**Khilafat** Campaign to protect the last link with the medieval caliphs (from which the name derives), meaning deputies of the Prophet Muhammad and leaders of the global Muslim community.

**Sultan** Muslim Arabic term indicating a regional political and religious leader – in this case the Ottoman emperor – but not claiming to be the supreme caliph.

## Chauri Chaura

And then at the height of the campaign, on 6 February 1922, Gandhi declared the movement over. He was personally devastated that, the day before, a protest mob in the town of Chauri Chaura had burned to death 22 policemen. For Gandhi the moral imperative was clear. A non-violent movement must be just that or nothing. He announced: 'Let the opponent glory in our so-called defeat. It is better to be charged with cowardice than to sin against God.'

For his supporters, both Hindu and Muslim, this was a betrayal of the movement. It left Congress split. The *Khilafatist* Muslims were even more demoralised when Turkish nationalists, led by Kemal Ataturk, swept to power in 1922, but promptly abolished the monarchy in the name of modernisation, leaving the sultan powerless and irrelevant.

Gandhi remained firm. Indeed, he declared his intention of removing himself from political campaigning, saying that he intended to work on regenerating the moral culture of India from his *ashram* at Sabarmati. On 10 March 1922, however, before he could devote himself to this programme, he was arrested by the British and charged with sedition.

**KEY TERM**

**Ashram** Small religious, often farming, community.

### SOURCE A

**From Gandhi's final address to the judge (Broomfield) at his trial, quoted in Mahatma Gandhi, *Young India 1919–1922*, B.W. Huebsch, 1924, pp. 1049–56.**

*In my humble opinion, Non-cooperation with evil is as much a duty as is co-operation with good … I am here, therefore, to invite and submit cheerfully to the highest penalty that can be inflicted upon me for what in law is a deliberate crime and what appears to me to be the highest duty of a citizen. The only course open to you, the Judge, is either to resign your post and thus dissociate yourself from evil, if you feel that the law you are called upon to administer is an evil and that in reality I am innocent; or to inflict on me the severest penalty if you believe that the system and the law you are assisting to administer are good.*

How does Gandhi defend his actions in Source A?

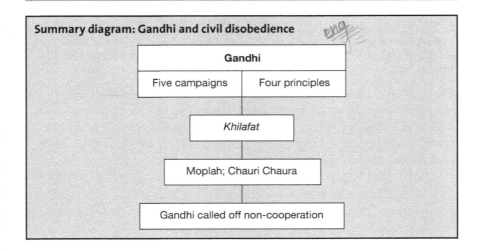

Summary diagram: Gandhi and civil disobedience

Gandhi
Five campaigns | Four principles

Khilafat

Moplah; Chauri Chaura

Gandhi called off non-cooperation

# The British response: control and concession

▶ *To what extent did the British move forward on constitutional reform?*

Despite the relative failure of the non-cooperation campaign of 1920–2, it was becoming clear to the British that Indian nationalism was developing and concessions would have to be made. The British recognised that Gandhi had become a (non-violent) force to be reckoned with. This is apparent in the tone of the judge's conclusion at his trial.

**SOURCE B**

**From the judgment by Broomfield, 18 March 1922, quoted in Mahatma Gandhi, *Young India 1919–1922*, B.W. Huebsch, 1924, pp. 1049–56.**

*There are probably few people in India, who do not sincerely regret that you should have made it impossible for any government to leave you at liberty. But it is so. I am trying to balance what is due to you against what appears to me to be necessary in the interest of the public. [The judge then justifies his sentence by comparison with the sentence passed on Tilak twelve years before.] You will not consider it unreasonable, I think, that you should be classed with Mr Tilak, … six years in all, which I feel it my duty to pass upon you, and I should like to say in doing so that, if the course of events in India should make it possible for the Government to reduce the period and release you, no one will be better pleased than I.*

If Gandhi's six-year sentence was intended to deter, it was too late. The Indian masses were no longer afraid of British legal authority. The arrest of tens of thousands during the campaigns had turned imprisonment into a badge of honour. Source C is a report of G.L. Watson, a district officer in the Central Provinces between 1932 and 1946.

**SOURCE C**

**Extract from a personal memoir by District Officer Watson, quoted in Roland Hunt and John Harrison, *The District Officer in India, 1930–1947*, Scolar Press, 1980, p. 189.**

*The [Congress] party secretary watched our [search of the local office] with obvious signs of unease but he probably was not altogether pleased when we left without arresting him. Jail was a recognized qualification for political office in the future. There was a young man in the district, who, I was told, would have paid 10,000r (£750) to be arrested.*

**?** What does Source B tell us about the conflicted British perception of Gandhi?

**?** Why do you think the young man in Source C wanted to be arrested?

## Indian participation in administration

Gandhi was released in 1924 on medical grounds (suspected appendicitis) and became president of Congress for a year. He was in no mood, however, for returning to national campaigning and retired to the *ashram* to concentrate on other matters. There had been widespread resignations from elected positions as part of the non-cooperation campaigns, although there was a significant body of opinion in Congress that this was counter-productive and that politicians should continue in office. This tension is sometimes referred to as the change/no change debate. Now, without Gandhi's leadership, or perhaps taking advantage of his absence, Indians resumed office in the various councils.

British Prime Minister David Lloyd George, speaking in August 1922, had angered Indians with a speech which undermined the Montagu Declaration (see page 26). He argued that the Indian Civil Service needed a core of British personnel as a building needs a steel frame to hold it up: 'Whatever we may do in the way of strengthening the Government of India, one institution we will not interfere with, will not deprive of its functions and privileges and that is the British Civil Service in India.'

In practice, however, the British system of provincial governance was changing. Source D has comments from Roland Hunt and John Harrison after their study of district officer memoirs.

### SOURCE D

**From Roland Hunt and John Harrison, *The District Officer in India, 1930–1947*, Scolar Press, 1980, p. 186.**

*Under varying degrees of official supervision, local politicians had also taken charge of the self-governing municipalities administering the town and the district boards in the rural areas. The district officer had to learn to share power with the politician. Moreover, the civil service itself was changing: since 1924 there had been no British recruitment to the professional and technical All-India services except the police, and more Indians were entering the Indian Civil Service … [C.S.] Venkatachar [district officer in United Provinces and Indian Political Service 1922–1960] argues that an irreversible shift of power occurred between 1919 and 1935: 'The politics of mediation between the people and the government had shifted … The politician now stood forward as the mediator and had displaced the district officer … The decline in the influence of the [district officer's] position was visible.'*

> What does Source D tell us about the shift in Indian involvement in provincial governance?

## The Muddiman Committee

It soon became apparent that there was discontent with the political system of dyarchy set up by the 1919 (Montagu–Chelmsford) Act (see page 31). In 1924 the Indian government set up a committee of inquiry, chaired by Sir Alexander Muddiman, a member of the government, which submitted its (split) report in 1925. The majority report agreed that the system was 'complex' and 'confused', but concluded that it was too soon to decide on more reform. The minority report declared that the system had 'no logical basis [and was] rooted in compromise and defensible only as a transitional expedient'. The secretary of state for India, Lord Oliver, criticised the reservation of seats for communal electorates in both the 1909 and 1919 legislation.

### SOURCE E

**From Lord Oliver, speaking in a House of Lords debate, quoted in *Hansard*, HL Deb, 26 February 1924, volume 56, columns 320–62.**

*This kind of discrimination between franchises is one of the things which are most dangerous to the unity of the British Empire. This principle I have held all my life, and if you want to disrupt and break up the British Empire the way to do it is to make this discrimination between one race and another on the ground of colour, and not on the ground of qualification.*

> **?** What fears does Lord Oliver raise in Source E?

In 1924 Lord Irwin was appointed as viceroy and Lord Birkenhead became secretary of state. Irwin would prove to be a skilful negotiator when Gandhi returned to political campaigning in 1930. Birkenhead made no secret of his antipathy to the Montagu–Chelmsford reforms. However, he also rejected the criticisms made in the minority Muddiman report and declared that the majority report showed that no change was necessary.

Nevertheless, a key feature of the 1919 reforms had been the promise of a review after ten years, scheduled for 1929. Birkenhead feared that, if the Conservative government was replaced by Labour in elections before then, concessions would be made to Congress and further reform would indeed follow.

## The Simon Commission

Accordingly, Birkenhead brought forward the review so that it could take place under his control. That control was evident in 1927 in his choice of people appointed to the review group, known as the Simon Commission after its chairman, Lord Simon. The commission did not contain a single Indian. So, before any discussion, let alone recommendation, it was clear that progress was unlikely.

When the Simon Commission arrived in India in 1928 on a fact-finding tour, the response of Congress was to boycott all meetings and hold protest demonstrations. The Muslim League, led by Jinnah, also avoided the commission. But the commission met other Muslim representatives, which Birkenhead publicised to try to disturb the Hindus and break the boycott.

The commission's work and eventual report was overtaken by two more radical statements: the Nehru Report and the Dominion Declaration. The Nehru Report will be examined in relation to Congress–Muslim League relations in the next section (see page 48). The British largely ignored it and it had no influence on the next legislation in 1935.

## The Irwin Declaration

The Simon Commission had never been likely to produce progressive findings, but Birkenhead laid down the limits anyway. He ruled out any reference to Dominion status, even as the ultimate goal of British policy, since this would concede the right of the nation to decide its own destiny and in his words: 'We were not prepared to accord India at present or in any way prejudice the question whether it should ever be accorded.'

Birkenhead may not have been prepared for that but his political instincts had been right. In 1929 a Labour government came to power and promptly announced plans for a round table conference. It also authorised the viceroy, Lord Irwin, to declare that: 'His Majesty's Government saw the attainment of dominion status as the logical outcome of the Montagu declaration of 1917.' British control would be retained over viceregal and military matters but provincial administration would be entirely Indian.

The defeated Conservative prime minister, Stanley Baldwin, supported the declaration in order to reassure Indian public opinion that it was agreed national policy and not a party-political tug-of-war.

Birkenhead, now no longer secretary of state, was outraged because the declaration (and the round table conference) pre-empted any recommendations of the Simon Commission and indeed rendered it irrelevant. More significantly for the future, the announcement roused the anger of Winston Churchill, the future wartime prime minister, whose opposition to Indian nationalism became as implacable as Gandhi's opposition to the British.

The Dominion declaration did nothing to hold back the growing radicalism of nationalism in India. Both the British and Congress were concerned by the growing strength of the **Communist** Party. The British response was to arrest and imprison the leaders for four years. Gandhi's tactic was to propel Jawaharlal Nehru, the socialist and Soviet sympathiser, to Congress leadership in order to avoid splits and challenges.

> 🔑 **KEY TERM**
>
> **Communist** The political philosophy of a supposed classless society with workers in power; ideology of the Soviet Union.

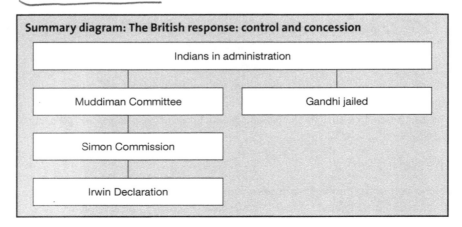

**Summary diagram: The British response: control and concession**

- Indians in administration
  - Muddiman Committee
    - Simon Commission
      - Irwin Declaration
  - Gandhi jailed

# Congress and the Muslim League

▶ *How did the demands of Congress and the Muslim League converge and diverge?*

Congress continued to dominate the nationalist movement and Gandhi dominated Congress although he was only briefly its president. It made demands of the British and mobilised popular protest. By contrast, the Muslim League felt uncomfortable with mass campaigns and saw its main objective as securing the principle of separate voting by Muslims and Hindus for protected numbers of representatives. The two groups had come together in the Lucknow Pact of 1916 but grown apart again and the influence of the Muslim League was declining.

## Muslim League reconciliation

The so-called Nehru Report (discussed immediately below) is the most well-known nationalist document of the decade. It has been identified by some historians as the point at which Congress rejected separate communal electorates as agreed in the Lucknow Pact. However, historian D.N. Panigrahi (commenting in *India's Partition*, 2004) points to the Delhi proposals of the Muslim League as counter-evidence. At a national conference in March 1927 of various Muslim groups but presided over by Jinnah, there was agreement on three matters which were in effect concessions or compromises:

1 *A joint electorate [that is not separated into Hindu and Muslim voters] in all provinces … provided that two new provinces of Sind and North West Frontier were created in Muslim majority areas with reciprocal arrangements for Hindu minorities if there were reservation of Muslim seats*

2 *In Punjab and Bengal representation (that is numbers of Hindus and Muslims elected) should be in proportion to the two communities in the local population*

3 *In the Central Legislature, Muslim representation to be not less than a third of the total but a joint electorate as in the provincial elections.*

These proposals were endorsed at the December 1927 meeting of the Muslim League. Panigrahi commends the 'enlightenment and foresight' of giving up separate electorates at both the provincial and central level. In other words, this was a significant gesture of reconciliation which must be considered as paving the way for the Nehru Report.

## The Nehru Report

The boycott of the Simon Commission had also drawn Indian political parties closer again. In 1928 an All Parties Conference was convened: an Indian-only round table conference. Representatives attended from Congress, the *Khilafat* Committee, Central Sikh League, the Indian (Princely) States' Subjects Association, the **Parsi *Panchayat***, the Bombay non-Brahmin Party, the Communist Party of Bombay and the Bombay Workers' and Peasants' Party.

The conference appointed a committee to draw up the principles of an Indian constitution under the chairmanship of **Motilal Nehru**.

After some difficulty, the Report of the Committee by the All Parties Conference to determine the principles of the constitution of India was presented in August 1928 to the fourth session of the All Parties Conference in Lucknow, which approved its recommendations. The recommendations included the following:

- joint mixed electorates for lower houses in central and provincial legislatures
- reservation of seats for Muslims on central councils and in minority provinces, with Hindu reservation in the North West Frontier Province
- no reservation of Muslim seats in the Punjab and Bengal
- reservation of seats for ten years only
- universal adult suffrage
- no state religion; freedom of conscience and practice of religion.

Some of these clearly matched the Muslim Delhi proposals. Such all-India agreement was encouraging to nationalists and the conference enthusiastically reappointed the committee to move on from this framework to the painstaking work of drafting a constitution which could be presented as a parliamentary bill. This proved a step too far. First, the idea of a bill was dropped and it was agreed that the report, slightly expanded, was impressive enough.

This may have been the result of internal Congress disagreement about the overarching recommendation that the nation would be called the 'Commonwealth of India' based on gaining Dominion status. Despite broad agreement, the radical wing of Congress, led by Jawaharlal Nehru (son of the chairman Motilal) and **Subhas Chandra Bose**, saw Dominion status as inadequate and the report as a disappointment. Nehru toured the country making rousing speeches demanding complete independence. He wanted a modern secular socialist state. Gandhi derided him and Bose as 'young hooligans'.

## Breakdown of relations

Then, at the All Parties Convention in Calcutta (late 1928 into 1929), Jinnah, speaking for the Muslim League, clashed with Jayakar of the All-India Hindu *Mahasabha*. Jinnah argued for preservation of the spirit of the Lucknow Pact (see page 23) by retaining Muslim reservation of seats in the Punjab and Bengal and one-third of the total seats in the central legislature. Jayakar urged the conference not to start undoing the report and questioned whether Jinnah was sufficiently supported by Muslim opinion.

**KEY TERMS**

**Parsi** Ancient Iranian religion.

**Panchayat** Assembly (originally of five village elders).

**Mahasabha** Translates as great association.

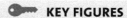

**KEY FIGURES**

**Motilal Nehru (1861–1931)**
Nationalist leader and father of Jawaharlal Nehru.

**Subhas Chandra Bose (1897–1945)**
One of the radical leaders within Congress, formed an Indian army in the Second World War to fight against the British.

At a subsequent meeting of Congress, the Nehru Report was warmly received, particularly by Gandhi. Jinnah told Congress that sympathetic statements were not enough: there must be legal protection of the position of minorities. He argued that concessions in order to preserve nationalist unity should come from the majority power, Congress, not the minorities.

When Congress rejected his arguments, Jinnah regarded it as a plan to exclude Muslims from the mainstream movement, prompted by their lack of united representation. Jinnah's hopes of an all-community nationalist movement faded. In March 1929 he made a counter-proposal for a federal constitution with protection for Muslims. This is sometimes called Jinnah's Fourteen Points, in a reference to US President Woodrow Wilson's post-war principles (see page 26). However, even the Muslim League rejected this direction. Jinnah decided to retire from politics and leave India for England.

**SOURCE F**

? How is the case made in Source F for retaining separate electorates?

**Resolution of the All-India Muslim Conference, Delhi, 1 January 1929, quoted in *Indian Statutory Commission Report*, volume 2, Cmd 3569, HMSO, 1930, appendix VII, pp. 84–5.**

*Whereas, in view of India's vast extent and its ethnological, linguistic, administrative and geographical or territorial divisions, the only form of Government suitable to Indian conditions is a federal system with complete autonomy and residuary powers vested in the constituent States, the Central Government having control only of such matters of common interest as may be specifically entrusted to it by the Constitution;*

*And whereas it is essential that no Bill, resolution, motion or amendment regarding inter-communal matters be moved, discussed or passed by any legislature, central or provincial if a three-fourth majority of the members of either the Hindu or the Muslim community affect thereby in the legislature oppose the introduction discussion or passing of such Bill, resolution, motion or amendment;*

*And whereas the right of Moslems to elect their representatives on the various Indian Legislatures through separate electorates is now the law of the land and Muslims cannot be deprived of that right without their consent;*

*And whereas in the conditions existing at present in India and so long as those conditions continue to exist representation in various Legislatures and other statutory self-governing bodies of Muslims through their own separate electorates is essential in order to bring into existence a really representative democratic Government; …*

## Purna swaraj

At the Lahore session of December 1929, Jawaharlal Nehru, as the new president of Congress, declared the goal of *purna swaraj* (total independence) and spurned the invitation to participate in the forthcoming round table conference.

Congress nominated 26 January 1930 as independence day. This proved to be the trigger for renewed non-cooperation with the hope of reuniting the nationalist movement while stemming support for the more radical movements led by Subhas Chandra Bose. The Congress working committee agreed at a secret meeting that Gandhi should have the freedom to initiate a civil disobedience campaign when he judged the moment right.

Gandhi, however, was not confident that the time was right for civil disobedience. He was worried about whether the masses would respond but also about the potential for violence. He inclined towards using a selected group of supporters chosen for their absolute, even religious, commitment to non-violence. Above all, he wanted to avoid Congress being held responsible for another Chauri Chaura (see page 43) and more accusations of betrayal if the campaign had to be halted.

## The Salt March

Gandhi's solution was brilliantly imaginative and has become one of the most famous protest events in history. He announced that, with 78 carefully chosen supporters, he would walk the 400 km from his *ashram* at Sabarmati to the sea at Dandi beach. The group would collect muddy sea-salt and boil it in order to make it pure and usable.

The apparent point of this campaign was to publicise a boycott of the salt tax, a tax by the British on a basic ingredient of cooking used by all Indians. However, Gandhi also wished, as he stated in a letter of intent to the viceroy: 'to convert the British people through non-violence and thus make them see the wrong they have done to India'.

At first, the British response was to treat the planned march as a joke. Then Gandhi held a gathering before the march which drew 75,000 people. On 11 March 1930, the day before the start, Gandhi himself addressed 10,000 at a prayer meeting. The British soon realised that the march was attracting world press attention.

*12 March 1930*

The 78 *satyagrahis* set out the next day. Every day, as well as marching about 20 km, they were expected to spin *khadi*, engage in group prayers, keep a diary and project peacefulness. If they encountered resistance they would submit according to the principles of *ahimsa*.

Accordingly, the march took on the character of a pilgrimage through the physical challenge and pain of walking in the heat of the sun in the hot dry season. The protest was hugely symbolic, did not threaten Indian economic interests and embraced all religious communities and castes. It appeared to pose no threat to the running of the British Indian Empire while drawing the world's attention to British greed and exploitation.

The Salt March also challenged the authorities as to how, or whether, to use force against such a peaceful, almost religious, event. On 5 April, the penultimate day of the march, Gandhi declared, 'I want world sympathy in this battle of right against might.' It was also noted, however, that Gandhi's own fear of tensions within the protest group had led to the exclusion of women and the inclusion of just two Muslims.

In towns along the route of the march, a large number of Indian officials resigned from their posts. Elsewhere, a march was organised in south India, there were protests in Bombay and the North West Frontier Province, and 2000 demonstrators at a salt production plant at Dharasana were attacked by police armed with *lathis* (steel-tipped canes). Two were killed and 320 injured. The international reporting of this showed the dangers of overreaction.

No direct action was taken against Gandhi and his *satyagrahis* when they reached the sea and the end of their march on 6 April. The police had been ordered to muddy up the salt deposits at the shore but this did not stop Gandhi creating a lump of salt that he auctioned for 1600 rupees (equivalent to £160 at the time).

The propaganda effect was running entirely in Gandhi's favour. Accordingly, the British felt compelled to take action, even if they managed to avoid an immediate overreaction. Over 20,000 protesters were arrested on the viceroy's orders and, on 4 May, Gandhi himself was arrested under a regulation of 1827 and taken to Yeravda jail in Bombay. If the British thought they had now neutralised Gandhi, they were sorely mistaken.

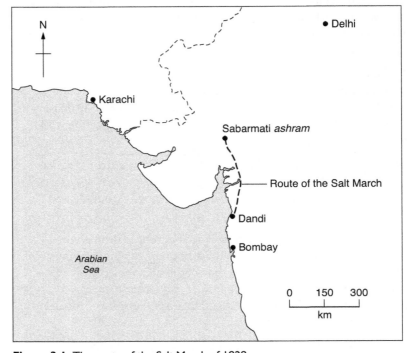

**Figure 3.1** The route of the Salt March of 1929.

**SOURCE G**

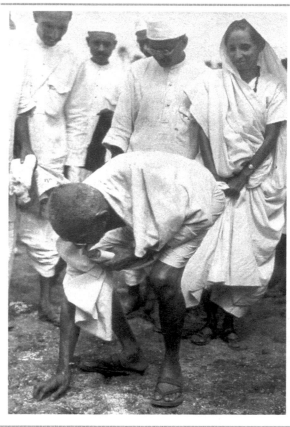

Gandhi at the end of his 1930s' Salt March. It is said that the photograph was staged three days after the march because the original beach was too muddy to see the salt.

Why is the moment captured in the photograph in Source H so important? **?**

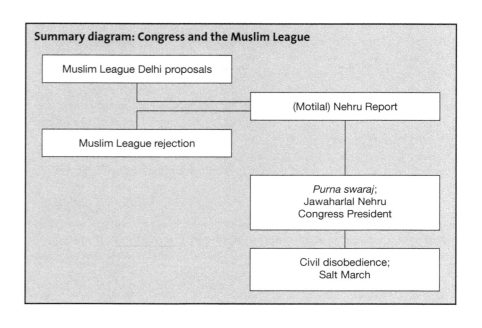

**Summary diagram: Congress and the Muslim League**

Muslim League Delhi proposals

(Motilal) Nehru Report

Muslim League rejection

*Purna swaraj*; Jawaharlal Nehru Congress President

Civil disobedience; Salt March

#  4 Key debate

▶ *How does the portrayal of the nationalist leaders by historians influence judgements about the ultimate success or failure of the independence campaign?*

The Indian independence struggle is, on the one hand, a sequence of dry constitutional arguments. Small surprise perhaps that historians have enlivened it, on the other hand, by dramatising the conflict between a few key individuals and their influence on the course of history. In one corner is Gandhi, a charismatic and inconsistent leader and thinker; in the other is Jinnah, less well known but still arguably the only man in history to create a brand new nation-state, Pakistan, simply by the force of his arguments. This debate contrasts the two figures and surveys historians' attitudes.

In his analytical memoir, *The Great Divide* (1985), H.V. Hodson, constitutional adviser to Viceroy Lord Linlithgow, precedes the main story with a chapter entitled 'Two Great Personalities' in which he contrasts Gandhi with Jinnah.

### EXTRACT I

**From H.V. Hodson, *The Great Divide*, Oxford University Press, 1985, pp. 34–5.**

*[Gandhi] had acquired a semi-divine aura, and to flout him had assumed the nature of a religious renunciation. But it was not only the saintly simplicity of his mode of life and attire that had earned him this political halo. His personality was one of remarkable power. Few Englishmen who met him were not charmed by him … To the British, even so, he was always an enigma – as indeed he remained even to his closest Indian associates – and many of them thought him two-faced and hypocritical. They contrasted his cult of non-violence with violent consequences that his satyagraha movements were bound to entail … They observed how often he had entered upon fasts unto death without dying … By nature, and in his conduct of life, [Jinnah] was cold, aloof and lonely. The scrupulous elegance of the Western clothes that he always wore, the monocle that he employed to transfix an audience of one or thousands, seemed deliberately to signal his apartness from the rest of the Indian world. Not even his political enemies ever accused Jinnah of corruption or self-seeking. He was a steadfast idealist as well as a man of scrupulous honour. The fact to be explained is that in middle life he supplanted one ideal by another, and having embraced it clung to it with a fanatic's grasp to the end of his days.*

The contrast is taken up by others: Gandhi's populism against Jinnah's lawyerish arguments; Gandhi's spirituality and rejection of Western values contrasted with Jinnah's preference for European codes of behaviour over Muslim ones (he drank alcohol, ate ham and rarely went to mosque).

These characterisations might influence readers' acceptance of judgements about the final outcome of the independence struggle. If the creation of Pakistan is seen as a success (for Muslims), then Jinnah is a national hero (in Pakistan). If partition is seen as the dismemberment of a unified India, Jinnah is a villain acting out of personal animosity against Gandhi, the all-loving peacemaker and national hero (in India).

The great champion of Jinnah, outside the subcontinent, is Stanley Wolpert, an American academic who holds no lingering regret for the end of the British Empire.

### EXTRACT 2

**From Stanley Wolpert, *Jinnah of Pakistan*, Oxford University Press, 1984, p. vii.**

*Few individuals significantly alter the course of history. Fewer still modify the map of the world. Hardly anyone can be credited with creating a nation-state. Muhammad Ali Jinnah did all three. Hailed as 'Great Leader' (Quaid-i-Azam) of Pakistan and its first governor-general, Jinnah virtually conjured that country into statehood by the force of his indomitable will. His place of primacy in Pakistan's history looms like a lofty minaret over the achievements of all his contemporaries in the Muslim League ... As enigmatic a figure as Mahatma Gandhi, more powerful than Pandit Nehru, Quaid-i-Azam Jinnah was one of recent history's most charismatic leaders and least known personalities. For more than a quarter century I have been intrigued by the apparent paradox of Jinnah's strange story ... in all the fascinating complexity of its brilliant light and tragic darkness.*

And yet, historian Patrick French has a different view of Jinnah.

### EXTRACT 3

**From Patrick French, *Liberty or Death*, Flamingo, 1997, p. 27.**

*[Jinnah is] the forgotten player in the story of India's independence and division. Neither side seems especially keen to claim him as a real human being, the Pakistanis restricting him to an appearance on the banknotes in demure Islamic costume. Generally he emerges late in the plot as a shadowy villain whose urge to create a Muslim homeland was motivated more by malice, spite and personal vanity than by statesmanship or a wish to protect the rights of a religious minority. In [final viceroy] Lord Mountbatten's phrase, which would probably have been endorsed by most of the Congress leadership in 1947, Jinnah was 'absolutely, completely impossible'. Even the apotropaic [evil-preventing] national hero Mohandas Gandhi described him as a 'maniac' and 'evil genius'.*

How does the choice of words and associations in Extracts 1–3 influence the reader's sympathies?

This is, therefore, not so much a debate about a particular event as an alert to the student of this period, particularly in reading more widely, that the choice of language used to represent decisions, motives and actions underpins the preferred judgement about the outcome. This is still very partisan historiography.

# Chapter summary

The start of the 1920s saw the eruption of mass political protest as a reaction to the Amritsar Massacre, the Rowlatt Act and anger at disappointing constitutional reward for the war effort. Gandhi led new forms of non-violent protest which exposed the British Empire's need for the co-operation of its subjects in maintaining power. Non-cooperation was treated as subversion. However, when protests became violent, Gandhi preferred to declare failure and defeat than to compromise his ideals. After imprisonment, he withdrew from campaigning.

For a brief period in 1927–8 there was the closest agreement between the two parties in the entire history of the independence struggle, evidenced in the congruent proposals of the Delhi Muslim conference and the Nehru Report, harking back to the Lucknow Pact of 1916. However, Jinnah argued that the pact had actually endorsed separate recognition of Muslim electorates (and this had been the principle of the 1909 and 1919 legislation). He overreacted and found himself isolated but the Nehru Report also foundered on criticisms of its lack of ambition for independence. Jinnah prepared to withdraw from politics and India; Gandhi launched his most imaginative protest.

#  Refresher questions

Use these questions to remind yourself of the key material covered in this chapter.

1 What were the key features of Gandhi's non-violent resistance strategy?

2 Why did Gandhi support the *Khilafat* movement?

3 What were the objectives of the 1920–1 campaigns?

4 What did Gandhi halt the campaign?

5 How did Gandhi and the British respond to his trial?

6 How was Indian involvement in local politics altering British administration?

7 How does the motivation behind the Simon Commission contrast with the substance of the Irwin Declaration?

8 How did the views of Congress and the Muslim League converge in the 1930s?

9 Why did they diverge?

10 Explain the significance of the Salt March.

# Question practice

## ESSAY QUESTIONS

1 'If Gandhi was horrified by the violence exercised from time to time by his followers, he longed to provoke it from those who had to be opposed by their non-violence.' How far do you agree with this statement?

2 How accurate is it to say that the British focus on Dominion status kept British and Indian politicians' attention away from solving questions of representation on councils?

3 To what extent did Jinnah sabotage the Nehru Report?

4 How significant was the Salt March in achieving Gandhi's objectives for *satyagraha*?

## SOURCE ANALYSIS QUESTIONS

1 Why is Source F (page 50) valuable to the historian for an enquiry into attitudes to communal electorates? Explain your answer using the source, the information given about it and your own knowledge of the historical context.

2 How much weight do you give the evidence of Source D (page 45) for an enquiry into the change from British district officers to Indian politicians in the administration of India? Explain your answer using the source, the information given about it and your own knowledge of the historical context.

3 How far could the historian make use of Sources A (page 43) and B (page 44) together to investigate the growing ineffectiveness of legal punishment in dealing with the nationalist movement? Explain your answer using both sources, the information given about them and your own knowledge of the historical context.

## CHAPTER 4

# Consultation and confrontation 1930–42

During the 1930s the British offered limited constitutional reform and protracted discussions were marred by disagreements among the Indian representatives. The 1935 Government of India Act offered hope of a federal India. Congress triumphed in elections to new provincial governments in 1937 and declined collaboration with the Muslim League. This set the League on a divergent path, with momentous consequences. Britain entered India into the Second World War, causing new political conflict. Federation was quietly dropped.

This chapter examines:

★ The round table conferences

★ The Government of India Act and its impact

★ Reaction to the outbreak of the Second World War

The key debate on *page 76* of this chapter asks the question: Did Jinnah really want to create Pakistan?

## Key dates

| | | | | | |
|---|---|---|---|---|---|
| 1930 | Nov. 12 | First round table conference | 1935 | Aug. 2 | Government of India Act |
| 1931 | March 5 | Gandhi–Irwin Pact | 1937 | | Indian general election |
| | Sept. 7 | Second round table conference | 1939 | Sept. 3 | Start of the Second World War |
| 1932 | Aug. 16 | British government's Communal Award | | Oct. | Resignation of Congress ministers |
| | Sept. 25 | Yeravda (or Poona) Pact | | Dec. 22 | Jinnah's Deliverance Day |
| | Nov. 17 | Third round table conference | 1940 | March | Lahore Resolution |
| 1933–4 | | Individual civil disobedience | | Aug. | Offer of post-war settlement |

#  The round table conferences

▶ *Why did the round table conferences fail?*

By the early 1930s the two main British political parties were Labour and the Conservatives. Labour was convinced that India was entitled to democratic autonomy. The Conservatives accepted the need for political concessions, if unrest threatened the Empire and white people in person, but they were generally content for progress to be slow.

On 31 January 1929 the viceroy, Lord Irwin, had announced that the government would convene a round table conference to settle India's constitutional future. This had been followed by the Irwin (Dominion) Declaration of October 1929 (see page 47). Indian nationalists naturally assumed that the objective of the conference was to draw up a Dominion constitution for India, especially as a new Labour government took power in June 1929.

The Liberals and Conservatives were generally opposed to the granting of Dominion status and the government stepped back. Lord Irwin explained to Gandhi, in prison, that the announcement of the conference had been merely to provide reassurance about long-term intentions and ensure co-operation with the Simon Commission. Dominion status would not be on offer at the conference. Later the same month, Congress responded by agreeing, at its meeting in Lahore, to the objective of *purna swaraj* and resolving to boycott the conference.

## The first round table conference

On 12 November 1930 the round table conference was convened in the House of Lords, London. The conference started with 89 representatives: sixteen from the three main British political parties, sixteen princes and 57 nominees of the viceroy to represent British India, including Muslims, Sikhs, Indian Christians and scheduled castes (termed depressed classes at the conference). Congress was denied any representatives because it had demanded a commitment to Dominion status as a precondition of its participation, which had been rejected. The Muslim League remained insignificant at this time.

The first session ended in January 1931 with a basic agreement on two points of a future constitutional settlement:

- Central and provincial executive power should be accountable to legislatures (as in modern democracies).
- British India and Indian India (the princely states) should be federally linked as one nation.

*The Times'* correspondent summed up the general realisation that 'no Indian delegation without Gandhi, the two Nehrus or Patel could possibly be looked on as representative'. Moreover, so long as Gandhi remained in prison he would be a focus, indeed a cause, of protest and rejection. Accordingly, in January 1931,

Irwin took the bold step of releasing Gandhi in order to undertake personal negotiations. These led to a political agreement which enabled the round table conference to progress but also led to accusations of betrayal on both sides.

## The Gandhi–Irwin Pact

The agreement was a formal legal document, signed on 5 March 1931 and publicised the same day. Known as the Gandhi–Irwin Pact, it stated that, on Gandhi's side, the civil disobedience movement would be halted and Congress would participate in a reconvened round table conference in return for British concessions such as release of political prisoners not guilty of violent crime, cancellation of fines, unbanning of organisations and permission for peaceful picketing in support of Indian goods.

Congress ratified the agreement, although there was criticism that yet again the mass movement had been abandoned when it seemed to be getting somewhere. However, the symbolism of a pact which treated Gandhi as the equal of the viceroy was more important than the detail.

Irwin, however, had recognised the dangers of ever larger and more effective mass movements. He reported to the British government that repression by force would only make matters worse in the long run. Political dialogue was the only safe way forward. He stated his view that: 'What is important is to make perfectly plain to India that the ultimate purpose for her is not one of perpetual subordination in a white Empire.'

## British reaction

To the British Conservatives it appeared that the government was rewarding the principal Indian troublemaker for creating disorder. Winston Churchill, later to become prime minister, was 'alarmed' when he spoke in the House of Commons in 1931 (see Source A).

### SOURCE A

**From Martin Gilbert, *Winston S. Churchill: Prophet of Truth 1922–1939*, quoted in Patrick French, *Liberty or Death*, Flamingo, 1998, p. 93.**

*[It is] alarming and also nauseating to see Mr Gandhi, a seditious Middle Temple lawyer, now posing as a fakir [a Muslim holy beggar] of a type well known in the East, striding half-naked up the steps of the viceregal palace while he is still organising and conducting a defiant campaign of civil disobedience to parley on equal terms with the representative of the King-Emperor. Such a spectacle can only increase the unrest in India and the danger to which white people there are exposed.*

Churchill resigned from his opposition **front-bench position** in 1931 specifically to campaign against Congress around Britain. Churchill had grown up surrounded by imperialist beliefs in the superiority of white people and Christian values. He now formed the India Defence League with support from

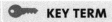

**KEY TERM**

**Front-bench position**
A post in the opposition party shadowing an actual government minister.

How does Churchill's choice of language convey his political views in Source A?

50 Tory MPs and Lancashire cotton industrialists. His reactionary passion led him to make statements such as that democracy was 'totally unsuited' to Indians. He saw no problem with making it clear to Indians that they would be forever subordinate subjects in a British Empire. This in turn led Prime Minister Stanley Baldwin to declare that the greatest danger to the Empire was 'extremists in India and at home'. By contrast, when Gandhi arrived in Britain for the second round table conference, he drew cheering crowds, even when he toured the Lancashire mill towns himself. In the east end of London he was told 'What this country needs is a few Gandhis.'

## The second round table conference

The round table conference reconvened on 7 September 1931, chaired by the new secretary of state, Sir Samuel Hoare. Gandhi was the only representative of Congress and was **mandated** to make no concessions from the demand of *purna swaraj.*

It was soon clear that questions of representation on the Indian side were a major source of contention. Gandhi claimed to speak for all India, bluntly questioning the right of his fellow Indians to be round the table at all. This naturally provoked anger from the three Muslim representatives and the representative of the scheduled castes, Dr Bhimrao Ambedkar, who stated: 'We, the Depressed Classes, demand a complete partition between ourselves and the Hindus … We have been called Hindus for political purposes, but we have never been acknowledged socially by the Hindus as their brethren.'

Gandhi agreed to chair the Minorities Sub-committee, but his son Devadas, who was in London with him, reported his despondency and suspicions in a letter to Nehru (see Source B).

### SOURCE B

**From a personal letter from Devadas Gandhi to Jawaharlal Nehru, 2 October 1931, Nehru Papers, Nehru Memorial Museum and Library.**

*He has no heart in the work of the Minorities Committee … In spite of this he has agreed to the Muslim request that he should call together representatives of the various groups in order to discuss the whole communal question. [He] has decided to give one week to these discussions after which he is going to have nothing to do with the question. If the discussions fail, as he fears they will, he intends to make a statement next week in the Minorities Committee giving a bit of his mind to the Government. He feels that the communal question is being brought deliberately to the forefront and magnified by the government because they did not intend to part with power … [He] feels that he has been deliberately saddled with the responsibility with a view to discrediting him when the whole thing ultimately fails as it is bound to do. He told the [prime minister, Ramsey MacDonald] that there was no meaning in bringing Dr Ambedkar here unless it was to create difficulties. He represented the depressed classes better than Dr Ambedkar. He expressed similar views about the other small minorities.*

 **KEY TERM**

**Mandated** Instructed by a political organisation or authority.

? Contrast the tactic in Source B with the 'divide and rule' strategy discussed in Chapter 1's Source B on page 10.

### The Communal Award and the Yeravda (Poona) Pact

Unsurprisingly, the second session ended without agreement. As a result, on 16 August 1932 the British government unilaterally announced the Communal Award setting out rights to separate representation for recognised minorities and for the scheduled castes. This last point provoked Gandhi to start another fast to death on the grounds that Congress, or at least he personally, was the best protector of the Dalits, whom he had taken to calling *harijans*.

Shortly afterwards, Congress leaders reached an agreement with Ambedkar in which the scheduled castes got more reserved seats in future elections but relinquished separate electorates. This agreement is known as the Yeravda or Poona Pact after the location of the negotiation. There were problems, however, as one participant in the third round table conference pointed out in Source C.

#### SOURCE C

**From a letter from Sir Tej Bahadur Sapru to Gandhi, 3 October 1933, quoted in the T.B. Sapru Papers, Nehru Memorial Museum and Library.**

*We cannot hope to achieve any great success without first solving our own internal problems. The fact that the Hindus and Mohamedans [Muslims] have not been able to come to a settlement and that there are some Hindus now who are expressing their dissent from the Poona Pact has materially affected the situation. I doubt very much whether there is any chance in the near future of coming to a communal settlement.*

## The third round table conference

By the time the third round table session was convened, in September 1932, Prime Minister Ramsay Macdonald had lost the support of his own Labour Party and continued in office only through a coalition National Government. The Labour Party did not send any representatives to the third conference and because it had been the main driver for Indian political progress, this doomed the final session to failure. Gandhi and many others did not attend.

## Civil disobedience

While Gandhi had participated in the second session of the round table conference, the repression of ordinary Indians had continued with particularly brutal measures in Bengal.

When the demoralised Gandhi returned from the second round table, Viceroy Willingdon had him arrested within a week of his return. Congress declared that the letter and spirit of the Gandhi–Irwin Pact had been broken and requested discussion with the viceroy. Congress resolved on 1 June 1932 to resume civil disobedience if it did not receive a satisfactory response. Instead, the government granted itself, within 24 hours, emergency powers. It proceeded to outlaw not Congress as such, but the whole of its working organisation, its

**SOURCE D**

**Gandhi at the round table conference in September 1931.**

Study Source D. Given the weather in London at the time, what would Gandhi's choice of clothing suggest to a British newspaper reader?

local branches and committees. An estimated 100,000 people were placed under immediate arrest. The confrontation of a year before was firmly back in place and Nehru described British India as a police state.

Gandhi, fasting in protest at the Communal Award, was released from prison on health grounds. He promptly advised Congress to end the civil disobedience and requested the government to release the prisoners. Both refused.

## Individual civil disobedience

Congress instead announced that individuals should feel free to take responsibility for their own civil disobedience. Between August 1933 and March 1934 thousands took such action while Congress could claim it was not official policy. Gandhi was again arrested but once again released because of his health.

Eventually, the action was crushed by mass arrests and repression, but the nationalist movement had lost its fear together with its respect for British justice and values. A *Guardian* newspaper correspondent wrote about protests just two years earlier (see Source E).

Moreover, it is clear from the private reports of various viceroys that the nationalists and their civil disobedience were having much greater success than anticipated and no one knew how to deal with Gandhi.

How do the actions and reactions in Source E relate to the Gandhian principles in Chapter 3?

**SOURCE E**

From *The Guardian* news article by H.N. Brailsford in 1931, quoted in P. Mehra, *A Dictionary of Modern Indian History 1707–1947*, Oxford University Press, 1987, p. 142.

*To face the* lathi *charges became a point of honour and in a spirit of martyrdom volunteers went out in hundreds to be beaten. They gave a display of disciplined passive courage. The great mass of the people is not in a normal state of mind. It has been roused to a high pitch of sustained … anger, it doubts our sincerity and above all it is passionately devoted to its imprisoned leaders.*

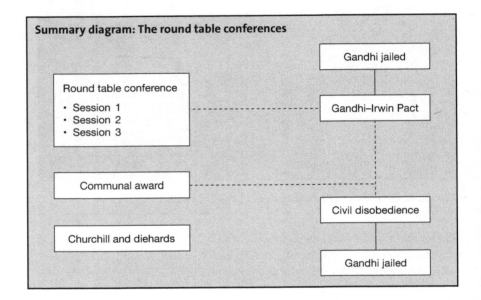

Summary diagram: The round table conferences

Round table conference
- Session 1
- Session 2
- Session 3

Gandhi jailed

Gandhi–Irwin Pact

Communal award

Churchill and diehards

Civil disobedience

Gandhi jailed

## 2 The Government of India Act and its impact

▶ *What was the impact of the Government of India Act?*

▶ *How did the 1937 elections change the direction of the political struggle?*

In 1917 Montagu had declared; in 1929 Irwin had announced. The Simon Commission and the round table conference had come and gone. Resentment in India continued to rise while political progress was stalled. Finally, in 1933 the British government published the long-awaited **white paper** on the Indian constitution.

The three main principles, based on such agreements as were reached at the round table conference, were as follows:

**KEY TERM**

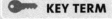

**White paper** A firm set of proposals for legislation.

- eventual **federation** at the national level
- provincial autonomy
- special responsibilities and safeguards vested in the executive power.

The white paper proposals were drafted as a bill by a joint select committee which included 21 delegates from British India and the Indian states and was chaired by Lord Linlithgow (soon to become viceroy).

## The Government of India Act

The Bill received royal assent on 2 August, becoming the Government of India Act 1935. With 450 clauses and fifteen schedules it was the longest and most complicated legislation ever passed by Parliament. Even then, it proposed to settle the extent of the franchise by subsequent **orders-in-council**. And despite all that, it still managed to avoid setting a date for Dominion status.

The main provisions of the Act, which would come into effect in 1937, were as follows:

- to expand the electorate to 35 million people (still less than ten per cent of the population)
- to abolish dyarchy and give provincial control to all matters previously 'reserved'
- to establish full provincial governments each with a legislature and executive
- to retain viceregal responsibility for defence and foreign affairs
- to separate off from 1 April 1937 the province of Burma (which would have its own governor reporting to London)
- to create two new provinces: Orissa and Sind
- to reserve emergency powers for central government, including overturning provincial legislation during 'disorder'.

### Nationalist response

The prolonged wait for further reforms again ensured that Indians would be disappointed by the outcome. As Nanda Saheb, a biographer of Gandhi, has commented: 'Each instalment tended to become out of date by the time it was actually granted. The reforms of 1919 might well have appeased India in 1909; the reforms of 1935 would have evoked enthusiasm in 1919, etc.'

In any case, the full effect of the Act would not come until elections in 1937 so there was a lull in activity. Congress in particular was divided between opposition to the Act in principle and attempting to gain whatever power the Act offered.

### Federation and the princes

A major feature of the Act was the aim of eventual federation of British India and the princely states, once half of them had agreed to the union. Although no date had been set for Dominion status, it was clear that it would come. So, the British attempted to ensure that a future self-governing Dominion had a constitution which would strengthen conservative and loyal elements, limit the control

**KEY TERMS**

**Federation** A national political grouping of regions with substantial autonomy.

**Orders-in-council** Legislation approved by a viceroy without full parliamentary scrutiny.

which Congress might seek and increase regional power which might weaken Congress as a national organisation.

Accordingly, along with concessions to the Muslim League, the federation of the princely states was designed to bring into government these conservative princes. To help persuade them, the Act contained various protections and inducements. For example, the princes would be permitted to select their own representatives without elections. In addition, although the princely states contained twenty per cent of the population, they would have 33 per cent of the representatives in the lower federal assembly and 40 per cent in the higher council of state.

Nevertheless, the princes refused one by one to sign up to the agreement. They feared that there would be pressure to move from their autocratic structures towards democratic processes and to relinquish their personal armies into national armed forces. Their opposition stalled any moves towards federation and when Britain declared war on Germany in 1939, the initiative was formally suspended.

Some historians, for example John Keay, regard the 1935 federation proposal as a major lost opportunity to hold India together; others such as H.V. Hodson dismiss it as never likely to have gained widespread support. Nehru observed ironically how eager the 'advanced' Europeans were to work with the most reactionary forces of 'backward' India to thwart progress. He clearly regarded it as a delaying tactic.

## Congress leadership

Gandhi remained the prime force within Congress despite not holding office. He observed that younger radicals such as Jawaharlal Nehru and Subhas Chandra Bose had increasing popularity and might pull Congress in a more radical direction. Gandhi had a backward-looking vision of a return to an almost medieval religious society, whereas Nehru had a modern socialist vision of an industrial economy and was zealously atheistic – his scorn for communal sensitivities would lead to bitter personal antagonism with Jinnah.

Gandhi's tactic was to ensure that they became Congress presidents in turn (Nehru 1929, 1930, 1936, 1937; Bose 1938, 1939). His hope was to tame them through the responsibility of holding Congress together, forcing them to consult and compromise, just as he had been made to do in the second round table conference. The strategy worked well with Nehru, who would later become the first prime minister of independent India, but not at all with Bose, who increasingly admired European fascist parties (see further below).

## The 1937 elections

The elections of 1937 electrified the political situation. Congress was victorious and was now, in effect, the governing party of India, whereas political representation for Muslims was fragmented:

- Congress took power in Bihar, Bombay, Madras, the United Provinces and the Central Provinces.
- It had 1500 representatives nationwide but only 26 were Muslims, less than two per cent.
- There were 482 seats reserved for Muslims and the Muslim League was the largest group, but with only 109 seats.
- Muslims formed 22 per cent of the national population but the Muslim League held fifteen per cent of all the seats.

Congress felt itself so powerful as a result of the electoral landslide that it refused to co-operate with the viceroy unless he promised not to overrule decisions by provincial governments. The disdainful Linlithgow was eventually forced to agree. But then Congress itself treated the Muslim League with disdain by refusing to form coalition provincial governments.

## The United Provinces stand-off

In the election for the provincial government of the United Provinces (actually a single British province), Congress had secured overall control, but it came under pressure to appoint non-Congress Muslim candidates for two ministerial positions in the provincial government. This was because it had only put up nine (Muslim) candidates for the 64 seats reserved for Muslim representatives but all its candidates had lost to other Muslim groups. The Muslim League had secured 27 of the seats, nearly half.

Although it was a provincial matter, Nehru blocked any concession from his position as Congress President. He justified this action as saving the dignity and loyalty of Muslims who worked for and within Congress. In her book *The Sole Spokesman* (1985), historian Ayesha Jalal has described the refusal to make any concession to the Muslim League as 'An assessment which seemed reasonable enough in the first flush of victory in 1937 but one which was to prove to be one of the gravest miscalculations by the Congress leadership in its long history.'

Nehru had consistently rejected communal politics because it had no place in free elections in a modern democracy. A progressive socialist party, such as he wanted Congress to be, should not get dragged back into such deals. Nehru could be very high-minded and forward-looking but his relationship with Jinnah could be personally barbed. He once declared that he came 'into greater touch ← like Gandhi with the Muslim masses than most of the members of the Muslim League'. This had echoes of Gandhi's arrogant claim to represent the scheduled castes better than one of their own.

In the view of Jalal (and many other non-partisan historians), the broader political consequences should have been foreseen and the Congress Muslims should have been denied the cabinet positions. Shutting out the Muslim League would only push them away from working with Congress. They would then turn to the British for stronger political protection. Muslim minorities

At the time, many could sense this because Nehru came under intense pressure within Congress to accept a compromise deal. Just when the details had been agreed, the Muslim League made a new surprising demand that Muslim League ministers working within a Congress provincial government should retain the right to vote against their own government if it was a communal matter. This was so clearly unacceptable (to any group forming a government) that it appears designed, by the Muslim League, to break the deal at the last minute. The closeness of agreement suggests a willingness to compromise; the deal-breaker suggests a political calculation that a divergent independent strategy was already contemplated by Jinnah.

D.M. Panigrahi, a pro-Nehru historian, points out, in his *India's Partition* (2004), that the Muslim League did, in fact, quietly move on without making a fuss of the United Provinces rejection. It was not until 1940 that Jinnah referred publicly to 'the betrayal' by Congress over the ministerial positions. By then the Lahore Resolution (in favour of independent states, see page 71) had been passed and, therefore, this reference to the 1937 fallout might be seen as a necessary later justification (in 1940) rather than an explanation of what the League was actually thinking in 1937.

## Consequences

### The Muslim League

Jinnah, who had been persuaded in 1935 to return from his successful law work in London to lead the Muslim League, had already reformed the structures of the Muslim League and appointed effective supporters to key positions. Following the 1937 defeats:

- Jinnah persuaded smaller Muslim organisations to merge with the Muslim League. Maulana Abul Kalam Azad, the leading Muslim within Congress, rejected this and Jinnah denounced him as a puppet of the Hindus.
- Knowing that political Muslims were generally of the landlord and landowner class, he did not emulate the social radicalism and working-class character of Congress in his leadership of the Muslim League. To further appeal to this class, he promoted the social use of the high-class language Urdu, even though he could not speak it himself.
- Despite his own belief in secular politics and states, Jinnah began to campaign openly on a separate Muslim basis rather than as part of a nationalist movement.
- Increasingly, Jinnah identified Congress as the threat to Muslim interests. A popular target was the Congress anthem, '*Bande Mataram*' (or *Vande Mataram*, 'I sing praise to thee, Mother [India]'), which praised most of the communities of India while pointedly not mentioning the Muslims.
- Finally, Jinnah increasingly moved from the objective of protected Muslim representation within India towards the objective of independent Muslim-

*Paraphrase*

controlled provinces or even states. The idea of a separate Pakistan appeared to be a useful negotiation point – whether as a promise to Muslims or a threat to Congress.

## Congress

In the eight provinces where Congress was in power, the party was naturally absorbed in the business and problems of (provincial) government. This had the effect of blunting the edge of further campaigning for independence, which had long been the strategy of some British reformers. In the three provinces where Congress was not in control, there was a tendency for Congress members to try to get others to ally themselves with Congress, so as to become the majority party, rather than operating as, for example, the official opposition party as in the British Parliament.

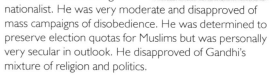

# Muhammad Ali Jinnah

| | |
|---|---|
| 1875 | Born in Karachi, in modern-day Pakistan |
| 1909 | Appointed as Congress Muslim representative on Imperial Legislative Council |
| 1913 | Joined the All-India Muslim League |
| 1919 | Resigned over the Rowlatt Act |
| 1929 | Presented the Fourteen Points |
| 1935 | Returned from London to lead the Muslim League |
| 1940 | The Lahore Resolution demanded the formation of independent states (Pakistan) |
| 1944 | Involved in the Gandhi–Jinnah talks |
| 1946 | Called for direct action as a result of the Calcutta killings |
| 1947 | Became governor-general of Pakistan |
| 1948 | Died |

Muhammad Ali Jinnah was born into a lower middle-class family. His father was a merchant. As a lawyer, Jinnah quickly developed a reputation for devastating effectiveness and gained great wealth as a result. His professional success, reflected in his sophisticated style of dress and manner, was an important part of his appeal to those middle-class Muslims able to vote. However, Jinnah's personal life was less happy. His first wife died at a young age. His second wife, Ruttie, was half his age and from a Parsi family, which caused family friction. Ironically, Jinnah would later disown his beloved daughter Dina when she married a non-Muslim.

Historians recognise two broad phases to Jinnah's political career. Up to the end of the 1920s Jinnah was a committed Congress nationalist. He was very moderate and disapproved of mass campaigns of disobedience. He was determined to preserve election quotas for Muslims but was personally very secular in outlook. He disapproved of Gandhi's mixture of religion and politics.

The Congress rejection of Muslim quotas in the Nehru Report drove Jinnah out of politics for a while. However, the Congress rejection of Muslim politicians after the 1937 elections spurred him to take control, at the request of many Muslims, of the All-India Muslim League. Increasingly, Jinnah appeared to support Muslim separatist demands. He started to learn Urdu, which was likely to become the official language of Pakistan, and appeared at public events in formal Muslim clothing. The culmination of this second phase of his career would see Jinnah, uniquely among modern politicians, create almost single-handedly a completely new state formed on a religious basis and become its first supreme leader.

Jinnah is often treated as the villain of Indian nationalism – the wrecker of a united independent India. Much of this comes from his lack of personal charm. Even a friend described him as 'tall and stately, formal and fastidious, aloof and superior of manner'. In Pakistan, however, he is revered as *Baba-e-Qaum* (Father of the Nation) and *Quaid-i-Azam* (Great Leader).

Gandhi became still more distanced from real politics. On the one hand, he thought the new powers likely to corrupt and distract Indian politicians. On the other, he regarded his own spiritual 'corruption' as responsible for the problems of the country. Jad Adams, in his study of Gandhi, describes how, in 1938, Gandhi was preparing for a crucial negotiation with Jinnah about Hindu–Muslim reconciliation when he was 'cursed by a uniquely Gandhian event' – he had an involuntary ejaculation. Gandhi immediately publicised his 'failure' and declared himself unfit to lead the negotiation.

To co-ordinate its approach across the country in the various provincial governments, Congress created the Congress Parliamentary Board (CPB) – in short, a party committee to determine national policy. The chairman of the CPB, Sardar Patel, was therefore the most important politician in the country. Patel ensured that the more radical proposals of the Congress president, Nehru, were aired but then defeated. In the words of a British intelligence report: 'Nehru is the high-grade tool in the hands of the skilled craftsman.'

Nevertheless, overall there was a palpable sense, within India, of Indians governing Indians. For the first time, the terms 'prime minister' and 'council of ministers' were used. Within a short period, ministries increased spending on education and public health, while regulating landlords and moneylenders. The ministries worked effectively, distributing and allocating work with little intervention or obstruction from British governors. Parliamentary secretaries were appointed to develop a new generation of political leaders. However, Hodson points out that much of this was not sensed back in Britain. As before, British political awareness was about ten years out of touch. This would be a crucial factor with the arrival of Churchill as war leader; all of this progress was about to be shattered.

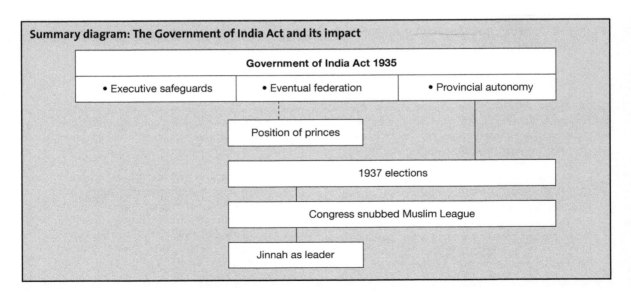

**Summary diagram: The Government of India Act and its impact**

| Government of India Act 1935 | | |
|---|---|---|
| • Executive safeguards | • Eventual federation | • Provincial autonomy |

Position of princes

1937 elections

Congress snubbed Muslim League

Jinnah as leader

#  Reaction to the outbreak of the Second World War

▶ *How did nationalist politicians respond to or exploit the British declaration of war?*

On 3 September 1939 the British prime minister, Neville Chamberlain, declared war on Germany. On the same day the viceroy, Lord Linlithgow, announced to the Indian people that they, too, were at war with Germany, without warning or consulting Indian political leaders.

The manner of the declaration was an affront to the self-respect of all Indians. Linlithgow declared that: 'confronted with the demand that she should accept the dictation of a foreign power in relation to her own subjects, India has decided to stand firm'. This no doubt sounded completely hypocritical to Indian ears. The British government, especially under the later leadership of Winston Churchill, appeared oblivious to the contradiction of fighting for liberty and democracy while attempting to thwart it for India.

## Indian reaction

Despite any misgivings, over 2 million Indians would join the armed forces to fight for the allied cause. Gandhi, meeting Linlithgow on the day after the announcement, was horrified that Britain was under threat. Both he and Jinnah agreed to halt all plans for federation (as laid out in the 1935 Act). Consistent with his views, Gandhi offered to meet Hitler on behalf of Britain to make peace and advised the British that complete **pacifism** was desirable.

Nehru and Congress had consistently condemned both fascism and British appeasement of it. They saw no need for sentiment or lectures on loyalty. Linlithgow's arrogant announcement caused great resentment and in October Congress instructed all its provincial ministers to resign.

Jinnah saw this as an opportunity for Muslims to put forward their demands and promptly and provocatively declared a Deliverance Day (from Congress/Hindu government) to be celebrated on 22 December. However, the Muslim League was in a tight situation. Source F recounts the report of Sir Harry Haig, governor of the United Provinces, to Viceroy Linlithgow.

## The Lahore Resolution

In Lucknow, after the 1937 elections, Jinnah declared his aim to be: 'the establishment in India of full independence in the form of a federation of free democratic states in which the rights and interests of the Musulmans [Muslims] were paramount'.

**🔑 KEY TERM**

**Pacifism** Refusal to fight in wartime.

What does Source F reveal about the trickiness of Jinnah's way forward?

**SOURCE F**

**From a letter from Sir Harry Haig, governor of the United Provinces, to Viceroy Lord Linthgow, 21 November 1939, Harry Haig Papers, India Office Library, London.**

*[Jinnah] said that if Congress decided on civil disobedience the Muslim League did not want either to leave the resulting struggle to be fought out between the British and the Congress or to take part in it merely as supporters of the British. They did not wish, on the one hand, to be charged with being 'toadies' nor, on the other hand, [to watch] a struggle by the British alone against the Congress at the end of which the British, if successful, might well say that they had no obligation to the Muslims who had not supported them … His conclusion was that the Muslims must fight this matter out themselves with the Congress [and] it would be over in a short time.*

At this point, therefore, what was envisaged was a federal India including Congress-dominated states, Muslim-dominated states and the princely states. In other words, taking the federation provision of the 1935 Act a step further to permit communal-majority states.

In January 1940 Jinnah wrote an article arguing for a new constitution because: 'There are in India two nations who both must share the governance of their common motherland.' He was deliberately raising the stakes by referring to Muslims as a nation rather than a community but not necessarily proposing two separate countries.

In March 1940 the biggest meeting to date of the Muslim League took place in Lahore. Sixty thousand gathered in a huge tent in Minto Park to hear Jinnah, dressed in traditional Muslim style, compare the situation of Hindus and Muslims to the relationship of the British and the Irish. He made the ringing declaration that: 'The Musulmans are not a minority. The Musulmans are a nation by any definition.' The Muslim League meeting passed the resolution shown in Source G.

### The hostage theory

The Lahore Resolution was denounced by Nehru as 'fantastic' and Gandhi called it 'baffling', a condescending dismissal since he too made grand, apparently impractical, demands as a political tactic. Perhaps the most important unanswered question was the consequences for the minorities left out. In the first place, there were many Muslims across India not in the concentrated areas of the north-west and north-east. Was it expected that they would move to the new states or would they become an even weaker minority in an almost total Hindu state? Similarly, declaring the Muslims to be a nation entitled to run their own country appeared to overlook the presence of other religious and ethnic minorities within those areas, notably Sikhs in the Punjab and Pathans in the North West Frontier Province.

**SOURCE G**

**From the Lahore Resolution of the Muslim League, 24 March 1940, quoted in**
***Parliamentary Papers X: India and the War* (1939–40), Cmd 6196, HMSO, 1940.**

What is being demanded in Source G?

*Resolved that it is the considered view of this Session of the All-India Muslim League that no constitutional plan would be workable in this country or acceptable to the Muslims unless it is designed on the following basic principles, viz: geographically contiguous units are demarcated into regions which should be so constituted, with such territorial adjustments as may be necessary, that the areas in which the Muslims are numerically in a majority as in the north-western and eastern zones of India should be grouped to constitute Independent States in which the constituent units shall be autonomous and sovereign.*

*That adequate, effective and mandatory safeguards should be specifically provided in the constitution for minorities in these units and in the regions for the protection of their religious, cultural, economic, political, administrative and other rights and interests in consultation with them; and in other parts of India where the Musulmans are in a minority, adequate, effective and mandatory safeguards shall be specifically provided in the constitution for them and other minorities for the protection of their religious, cultural, economic, political, administrative and other rights and interests in consultation with them.*

Jinnah's response came to be known as the hostage theory. This argued that the presence of residual minorities within both Hindu India and Muslim Pakistan(s) would force each majority to protect the rights of the minorities within their country for fear of reprisals against their co-religionists 'left behind' in the other country.

## The idea of Pakistan

In 1930 the prominent poet Muhammad Iqbal had proposed allowing Muslims and Hindus their own areas within one Indian state. The idea was crystallised in the name Pakistan, which allegedly came to Choudry Rahmat Ali while on a London bus. On the one hand, the name means 'land of the pure'; on the other, the letters are extracted from the names of the Muslim majority provinces: Punjab, Afghan (North West Frontier) Kashmir, Sind and Baluchistan. Significantly, Bengal is missing – it was perceived as a poor area, geographically inconvenient and full of converts from the Hindu 'Untouchables'.

The idea circulated in pamphlets without being taken seriously by either Indians or the British. The practical way forward seemed to be the reservation of seats for Muslims and other minorities as incorporated in British legislation in 1909, 1919 and 1935 and supported by Congress at the Lucknow Pact of 1916. However, the Nehru Report of 1928, and the Congress refusal after the 1937 elections to enter negotiations over ministers, showed that this position was precarious in any future Congress-dominated, independent India. Muslims and others would increasingly have to compete in open democratic processes.

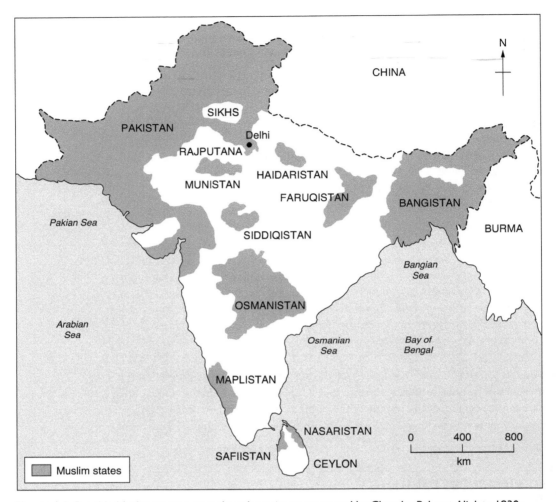

**Figure 4.1** Possible Muslim states across the subcontinent, suggested by Choudry Rahmat Ali, late 1930s.

## August 1940 offer

In 1940 the war was looking disastrous and the British government reached for a new leader: Winston Churchill. Churchill's reactionary views on India were well known but one of his previous critics, Leo Amery, was persuaded to become secretary of state. under Churchill (1940)

Amery attempted to clarify and settle matters by announcing in the House of Commons that Indian constitutional reform would be resumed after the end of the war. Since this implied nothing before the end of the war, it aroused little support. Linlithgow suggested to the war cabinet a slightly more specific offer of guaranteed steps towards Dominion status starting one year after the end of the war but ignored the need for a constituent assembly for democratic approval.

Churchill was personally against any sort of concession or declaration but eventually permitted Linlithgow to announce in August 1940 the idea of a post-war constitutional settlement. Too little, too late again, this was rejected by Congress, which was looking beyond Dominion status. Linlithgow warned the provincial governments that he would crack down heavily on Congress if it initiated civil disobedience, which it duly did, calling for individual actions again rather than a mass national campaign.

Swathes of arrests followed and some 20,000 Indians were imprisoned within a year. Linlithgow asked for emergency powers to declare Congress an illegal, even potentially treasonable, organisation. Although Churchill refused, he liked Linlithgow's hard-line approach and asked him to continue as viceroy beyond the normal term of office.

## Bose and the Indian National Army

The question of treason was more stark in the case of the Indian National Army (INA), formed and led by Subhas Chandra Bose, the former Congress leader.

In 1941 Bose was under house arrest, having recently been released from prison. He took the decision to leave India in order to fight for its independence from abroad. In disguise with false papers, he was smuggled out to Afghanistan and then travelled to Berlin where he met fascist leaders such as Ribbentrop and Mussolini, recruited a few thousand Indian prisoners of war (out of 17,000 in Europe) to his Indian legion and held marches behind a newly designed flag. He established the Free India Centre and made radio broadcasts in Indian languages.

After meeting Hitler, Bose realised the Nazis were more interested in this propaganda work than in unrealistic ideas about invading India and so he took up the offer of submarine passage to Japan in 1943. There he found the Japanese leader General Tojo more supportive.

Again Bose made propaganda broadcasts ending with the slogan *Dilli Chalo!* ('On to Delhi!'), the cry of the mutineers in 1857. Across the Far East, Bose was able to recruit from 2 million Indian prisoners of war. Ten thousand volunteered →who fought for the British overseas for the INA, although many did so to escape brutal prisoner-of-war camps. Many were desperate to get back to India because of the famine affecting Bengal from 1943 onwards, and managed to cross over to the British forces as soon as they could.

Eventually, the INA membership reached somewhere between 15,000 and 50,000, including a complete women's regiment. They were sent into action against the British in Burma. However, they were despised by their Japanese allies, pitifully supplied and armed, and were decimated. Thousands surrendered then, with complete surrender following the capture of Rangoon in 1945. Bose escaped to the island of Taiwan, but died in an air crash in August 1945.

Bose and the INA were never really a military danger, although it turned out that the British had underestimated their military strength. The threat came from their power to provoke unrest within India itself both during the war and afterwards, when the question arose as to how to deal with captured INA soldiers (see Chapter 5).

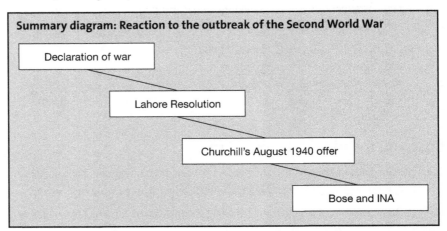

**Summary diagram: Reaction to the outbreak of the Second World War**

Declaration of war

Lahore Resolution

Churchill's August 1940 offer

Bose and INA

# 4  Key debate

▶ *Did Jinnah really want to create Pakistan?*

The focus of this debate is Jinnah's political strategy from 1937 onwards. The final outcome was the creation of Pakistan. However, the debate examines whether that was the objective all along or whether the demand for Pakistan was intended as a negotiating position to gain a better solution in a united India. This is, of course, a highly sensitive matter since the latter conclusion implies that Pakistan itself is a mistake of some sort.

The Lahore Resolution is, in the view of historian Asim Roy, the dividing line between orthodox and revisionist interpretations. The orthodox historiographical view is attributed principally to Stanley Wolpert in his book *Jinnah of Pakistan*.

### EXTRACT 1

**From Stanley Wolpert, *Jinnah of Pakistan*, Oxford University Press, 1984, p. 182.**

*Jinnah and his party were no longer willing to retain mere 'minority' status and the capital of the Punjab had been chosen purposely as the place to announce the Muslim League's newborn resolve … Jinnah did not use the name Pakistan nor would it appear in the forthcoming Lahore resolution. He had nonetheless obviously given much thought not simply to this immediate 'solution' for the Hindu–Muslim problem but also to the long-range international implications of partition. Jinnah no longer questioned either the wisdom, viability or the aftermath impact of partition but had decided by the spring of 1940 that this was the only long-term resolution to India's foremost problem … Those who understood him enough to know that once his mind was made up he never reverted to any earlier position realized how momentous a pronouncement their Quaid-i-Azam had just made … The ambassador of Hindu–Muslim unity had totally transformed himself into Pakistan's great leader.*

In this view, Jinnah comes to the rational conclusion that separation is inevitable and should be boldly seized as an opportunity. In addition, it would be more likely to succeed as a demand of the British as part of independence negotiations than as a later secession from a wholly independent India. The counterpart of this view is that Congress is positioned as the defender of a united independent India. Ultimately, Jinnah defeats Congress and emerges, in consequence, as either a villain (in India) or hero (in Pakistan).

Asim Roy approves the revisionist view, represented (but not created) by Ayesha Jalal in her book *The Sole Spokesman* and 'corroborated' by subsequently released private papers of Maulana Azad, the principal Muslim leader within Congress.

### EXTRACT 2

**Asim Roy, 'The High Politics of India's Partition: The Revisionist Perspective', Chapter 6 of Mushirul Hasan, editor, *India's Partition*, Oxford University Press, 1994, p. 110.**

*The revisionist view … envisages no real change in Jinnah's political goals but in his political strategies. His aims still continued to be to secure Muslim interests 'within' and not in total separation from India. It is simplistic, in this view, to take [the Lahore Resolution] as a final commitment to partition or Pakistan, if the latter term is used … not in Jinnah's special sense of being a strategically important embodiment of the Muslim claim of being a nation … The thrust of Jinnah's political strategy underpinning the resolution was initially to secure the recognition of the Indian Muslim nationhood on the basis of acceptance of the 'Pakistan' demand by the British and Congress and thereby gain an equal say for Muslims in any arrangement about India's political future at the centre. Once the principle of the Muslim right to self-determination, as embodied in the Lahore Resolution, was conceded, the resultant Muslim states or states could either 'enter into a confederation with non-Muslim provinces on the basis of parity at the centre' or make as a sovereign state, 'treaty arrangements with the rest of India about matters of common concern'. The resolution, in this sense, was, therefore nothing more than a 'tactical move' and a 'bargaining counter'.*

In this view, Jinnah understands that separation at the wings of the subcontinent will leave as many Muslims inside India (see the hostage theory). His ultimate objective is neither partition nor one single democracy (in which the Muslims are always outvoted) but a federal state with a patchwork of Congress-dominated regions, Muslim provinces and princely states. To achieve this, he raises the spectre of partition in order to pressurise Congress (and the British) into meaningful negotiations, leading to a compromise (federation) which they can present as successfully preserving India but which protects Muslim interests all across the land.

The orthodox view denies that Jinnah was not serious about Pakistan and was prepared to use the idea of Pakistan without really wanting to achieve its creation. That seems to be too sly and ignoble. The orthodox view therefore embraces what Roy defines as: 'the twin partition myths locked in a symbiotic relationship: "The League for partition" and "the Congress for unity" '.

### EXTRACT 3

**From Asim Roy, 'The High Politics of India's Partition: The Revisionist Perspective', Chapter 6 of Mushirul Hasan, editor, *India's Partition*, Oxford University Press, 1994, p. 106.**

*In the orthodox view, the resolution … was the first official pronouncement of the 'Pakistan' or 'partition' demand by the party. Though the term 'Pakistan' is nowhere to be found in the resolution, it is, nonetheless, seen to have provided for the separation of the Muslim majority areas in the north-western and eastern zones of India as 'sovereign' and 'independent states' and thereby formed the basis of the 'Pakistan demand'. Along with this perceived reformulation of the League's political objectives, there is also, intrinsic to this view, an equally significant assumption of a major turn and break in Jinnah's political development: the Islamization of the 'nationalist' and 'secular' Jinnah [and] Likewise, the Indian nationalist component of this historiographical orthodoxy has been content to project partition as the tragic finale of a heroic struggle of the Indian patriots against the sinister Machiavellian forces out to destroy the sacred Indian unity.*

? Study Extracts 1–3. Do you think the demand for Pakistan was a bargaining position?

The revisionist view sees Jinnah's speeches as ambiguous and cautiously incremental. The revisionists cite a number of problems for the orthodox case arising from the Lahore Resolution:

- The word Pakistan is conspicuously omitted from the resolution.
- There is no satisfactory explanation of the 'sacrifice' of Muslim minority areas to achieve the Muslim majority areas.
- Even the majority areas are plainly weak and unviable, especially imagined as two parts of one country, 1400 km apart.

In addition, they argue that Jinnah was simultaneously trying to stop strong regional leaders within the Muslim League, such as Fazlul Huq in Bengal, from campaigning for their own breakaway states.

The orthodox historians, whether they approve of Pakistan or not, credit Jinnah with a great achievement. The revisionist view is more subtle: they give him credit for the attempt at an even more complex strategy, which ultimately failed, namely to argue for a separate country in order to gain stronger protection for the Muslims in an undivided but looser Indian state.

In the revisionist view, Congress 'called Jinnah's bluff and shattered his strategy'. It was Nehru who rejected the cabinet mission plan and Azad's released correspondence identifies the influence on him of Viceroy Mountbatten. But in doing so, Congress embraced partition and is to blame for the dismemberment of India: a very controversial conclusion.

## Chapter summary

This period includes crucial developments in the independence movement, some successful, others failures which proved instructive. The attempt to bring everyone around the conference table failed, first because the British tried to ignore Congress and Gandhi and, second, because when Gandhi was included he elevated himself to the position of spokesman for all India's minorities.

The Government of India Act was uninspiring to Indians although it included an opportunity to create a federated India which might have prevented partition but which was brought down by the delaying tactics of the Indian princes and shelved at the start of the war.

The 1937 elections proved Congress's dominance of the political scene and the relative weakness of the Muslim League. Nehru was ascending as Gandhi was fading into faddism. Jinnah, working as a lawyer in London, was persuaded to save the Muslim League from obscurity after 1937. He demanded recognition of the Muslim nation in India and would become a forceful national leader over the next five years.

So too would Churchill, who loved the British Empire but hated Indians. Meanwhile Bose, the former young hooligan comrade of Nehru, hated the Empire so much that he worked with the Japanese enemy.

##  Refresher questions

Use these questions to remind yourself of the key material covered in this chapter.

1 What were the successes and failures of the first round table conference?

2 What was the significance of the Gandhi–Irwin Pact?

3 Why was Gandhi's inclusion in the second round table conference not productive?

4 What was resolved by the Communal Award (Yeravda Pact)?

5 Why and how was civil disobedience organised in 1932?

6 What were the main features of the Government of India Act 1935?

7 What was the significance of the federation proposal?

8 What was Jinnah's argument for provincial power sharing after the 1937 elections?

9 What was Nehru's reason for refusing?

10 What was the Indian response to the outbreak of the Second World War?

11 What was the 1940 offer?

12 How did Bose seek support for Indian independence?

13 How did Jinnah's political demands develop in the period 1937–42?

14 What was the key feature of the Lahore Resolution?

# Question practice

## ESSAY QUESTIONS

1 To what extent did disagreements among Indian nationalists destroy the hopes for the round table conferences?

2 'Nehru's rejection of attempts to share power in the provincial government of United Provinces was a strategic error in achieving the aim of a united, independent India.' How far do you agree with this statement?

3 How accurate is it to say 'The League for partition; the Congress for unity'?

4 How far did Jinnah's political strategy change in the years 1937–40?

## SOURCE ANALYSIS QUESTIONS

1 Why is Source 1 valuable to the historian for an enquiry into the dilemma of the Muslim League? Explain your answer using the source, the information given about it and your own knowledge of the historical context.

2 How much weight do you give the evidence of Source 2 for an enquiry into the causes of the failure of the round table conferences? Explain your answer using the source, the information given about it and your own knowledge of the historical context.

3 How far could the historian make use of Sources 3 and 4 (page 81) together to investigate Churchill's attitudes to Indian nationalism? Explain your answer using the sources, the information given about them and your own knowledge of the historical context.

---

**SOURCE I**

**From a letter from Sir Harry Haig, governor of the United Provinces, to Viceroy Lord Linthgow, 21 November 1939, Harry Haig Papers, India Office Library, London.**

*[Jinnah] said that if Congress decided on civil disobedience the Muslim League did not want either to leave the resulting struggle to be fought out between the British and the Congress or to take part in it merely as supporters of the British. They did not wish, on the one hand, to be charged with being 'toadies' nor, on the other hand, [to watch] a struggle by the British alone against the Congress at the end of which the British, if successful, might well say that they had no obligation to the Muslims who had not supported them … His conclusion was that the Muslims must fight this matter out themselves with the Congress [and] it would be over in a short time.*

---

**SOURCE 2**

**From a personal letter from Devadas Gandhi to Jawaharlal Nehru, 2 October 1931, Nehru Papers, Nehru Memorial Museum and Library.**

*He has no heart in the work of the Minorities Committee … In spite of this he has agreed to the Muslim request that he should call together representatives of the various groups in order to discuss the whole communal question. [He] has decided to give one week to these discussions after which he is going to have nothing to do with the question. If the discussions fail, as he fears they will, he intends to make a statement next week in the Minorities Committee giving a bit of his mind to the Government. He feels that the communal question is being brought deliberately to the forefront and magnified by the government because they did not intend to part with power ... [He] feels that he has been deliberately saddled with the responsibility with a view to discrediting him when the whole thing ultimately fails as it is bound to do. He told the [prime minister, Ramsey MacDonald] that there was no meaning in bringing Dr Ambedkar here unless it was to create difficulties. He represented the depressed classes better than Dr Ambedkar. He expressed similar views about the other small minorities.*

---

**SOURCE 3**

**From Winston Churchill's speech in Parliament during the second reading of the Government of India Bill, 11 February 1935, quoted in *Parliamentary Debates HC*, volume 297, HMSO, 1935, columns 1650–63.**

*We are invited to believe that the worst self-government is better than the best good government ... Yet it is those very functions which we have discharged and are discharging in India that have given India its immunity from the perils, the anxieties, the disorders and the burdens which oppress the strongest and most civilized nations in Europe. That is not the principle of self-government. It is the principle of beneficial aid from an external source for a virtuous object ... In so far as [British protection and security] are withdrawn and this external aid withheld, India will descend, not quite into the perils of Europe but into the squalor and anarchy of India in the sixteenth and seventeenth centuries ... We hope once and for all to kill the idea that the British in India are aliens moving, with many apologies, out of the country as soon as they have been able to set up any kind of governing organism to take their place ... We are there for ever as honoured partners with our Indian fellow subjects whom we invite in all faithfulness to join with us in the highest functions of government for their lasting benefit and for our own.*

---

**SOURCE 4**

**From a radio broadcast by secretary of state for India, Sir Samuel Hoare, 1 January 1935, reprinted in Sir Samuel Hoare, *Speeches by the Rt. Hon. Sir Samuel Hoare, 1931–1935*, Eyre & Spottiswoode, 1935, p. 135.**

*I certainly do not suggest that self-government is, in itself, preferable to good government ... But I do maintain that the old system of paternal government, great as have been its achievements on behalf of the Indian masses in the past, is no longer sufficient ... We have reached the point when the welfare of the people depends upon cooperation between the Government and political elements of the country and when the most difficult social questions such as the status of women and child marriage can only be settled by Indians themselves ... For 15 years many of the subjects that most directly affect the vital interests of the workers such as health and education have been in the charge of responsible [Indian] Ministers. Lord Salisbury and Mr Churchill do not propose to withdraw the departments that are already in Indian hands, indeed they profess to be willing to transfer practically all the subjects that affect the daily lives of the Indian masses. Why then do they attack us as if we were sacrificing the interests of the masses to Indian politicians and as if they were seeking to preserve and safeguard them?*

## CHAPTER 5

# The road to independence 1942–7

Nationalists were increasingly angered by the attitude of Churchill, the British wartime leader, who was opposed to further political progress for India. Congress demanded that the British leave India immediately, and politicians were imprisoned for preparing civil disobedience in wartime. Congress ordered a complete withdrawal from government. This provided an opportunity for the Muslim League to gain political prominence and appear more loyal. The surprise election of a Labour government in Britain at the end of the war ensured that independence would be granted to India.

This chapter examines:

★ The Cripps mission

★ The Quit India campaign

★ Viceroy Wavell

★ Attempts at political settlement 1945–6

## Key dates

| | | |
|---|---|---|
| 1941 | **Aug.** | Atlantic Charter supported self-government |
| 1942 | **April** | The Cripps mission |
| | **Aug. 8** | Quit India resolution |
| 1943 | | Suppression of political campaign |
| | **Oct.** | Wavell appointed as viceroy |
| 1943–4 | | Bengal famine |
| 1945 | **June 25** | Simla Conference |
| | | Indian general election |
| | **July** | British general election |

| | | |
|---|---|---|
| 1945 | **Aug. 9** | End of the Second World War |
| 1946 | | Indian general election |
| | **April** | Cabinet mission |
| | **May** | Simla Conference |
| | **May** | Cabinet mission's May statement |
| | **Aug. 16** | Direct Action Day |
| | **Sept. 2** | Interim government took power |
| | **Dec. 7** | Constituent assembly convened |

# 1 The Cripps mission

▶ *Why did the Cripps mission fail?*

## The war situation

At the start of 1942 the war was still going badly for the British. Then came a series of major losses in the East. The most traumatic was the surrender of the fortress city of Singapore. Japanese armies swiftly occupied British territory in Malaya and Burma. They were pressing at the north-eastern border of India itself. It was quite possible that the mighty British Empire would be conquered.

Churchill was acutely aware that Britain's survival rested on the strategic support of the USA. The US president, Franklin Delano Roosevelt, had from the start argued with Churchill about the situation of India (see below). It was more than just a matter of protecting the military position by avoiding unrest in India. It was the question of the purpose of the war which Indian nationalists had themselves raised. In a sense, Churchill was to find himself fighting a political war on two fronts: in India and in the USA.

### The Atlantic Charter

In August 1941 (even before the USA entered the war) Churchill and Roosevelt had agreed the basis of their co-operation in the Atlantic Charter which included support for 'sovereign rights and self-government'. The two interpreted this differently, however. Churchill regarded sovereign rights as applying to countries which had been conquered, whereas the *status quo* would apply to Britain and its empire. Roosevelt saw it as a fundamental principle applying to all. Accordingly, he consistently pushed Churchill to make concessions to Indian nationalist demands.

In response, Churchill blustered about morale in the Indian Army and the danger of promises but, in March 1942, agreed that the war cabinet should announce that the lord privy seal, Sir Stafford Cripps, would be sent to India to discuss the implications of the declaration on Dominion status made in August 1940. Roosevelt kept up the pressure as in, for example, his private message at the time of the Cripps mission, shown in Source A.

## Cripps' proposals

Cripps travelled immediately to India and stayed throughout March, meeting political representatives. His first assessment was bleak: 'unrest is growing amongst the population. The food situation is causing disquiet. The outlook so far as the internal situation goes is exceedingly bad.'

What warning is Roosevelt giving Churchill in Source A?

## SOURCE A

**Extract from a private message to Prime Minister Churchill from President Roosevelt, 12 April 1942, quoted in Winston S. Churchill, *The Hinge of Fate*, Houghton Mifflin Harcourt, 1986, p. 193.**

*I regret to say that I am unable to agree with the point of view contained in your message to me, that public opinion in the United States believes that negotiation has broken down on general broad issues. Here the general impression is quite the contrary. The feeling is held almost universally that the deadlock has been due to the British Government's unwillingness to concede the right of self-government to the Indians notwithstanding the willingness of the Indians to entrust to the competent British authorities technical military and naval defence control. I feel that I am compelled to place before you the issue very frankly and I know you will understand my reasons for doing this. Should negotiations be allowed to collapse because of the issues, as presented to the people of America, and should India subsequently be invaded successfully by Japan with attendant serious defeats of a military or naval character for our side, it would be hard to over-estimate the prejudicial reaction on American public opinion … I still feel that … the component groups in India could be given now the opportunity to set up a Nationalist Government in essence similar to our own form of government.*

# Winston Spencer Churchill

| | |
|---|---|
| 1874 | Born in Blenheim Palace, near Oxford |
| 1897 | Served as an army officer on the North West Frontier |
| 1899–1902 | Saw action in the Boer War, South Africa |
| 1900 | Became a Conservative MP |
| 1905–15 | Served as a Liberal government minister |
| 1914–18 | Saw action on the Western Front and became secretary of state for war |
| 1924–9 | Chancellor of exchequer in the Conservative government |
| 1940–5 | Prime minister during the Second World War |
| 1950–5 | Re-elected prime minister |
| 1965 | Died and given a state funeral |

Churchill was another of the great figures of the twentieth century. He was born at Blenheim Palace, awarded to his ancestor the Duke of Marlborough for military victories, but he was also the grandson of an American millionaire. He had a speech impediment, did poorly at Harrow public school and suffered from deep depressions.

Churchill threw himself into military action on the borders of the British Empire, combined with journalism. He entered Parliament as a Conservative but switched to the Liberals and soon held high office. He switched back after the war but his opposition to Indian nationalism and his calls to prepare for war against Germany, as well as the changes of party, gave him the reputation of a maverick.

The onset of war vindicated Churchill and he became an inspirational leader but he lost the 1945 elections because of popular desire for a more equal society. He became prime minister again in 1950 and was knighted in 1953. Later, US President Kennedy made him the first ever honorary US citizen. On his death, Queen Elizabeth II granted him a state funeral that was broadcast on television around the world.

Cripps had two parts to his brief:

- to explain and win backing for the August 1940 declaration by discussing the processes necessary to bring about Dominion status
- to discuss arrangements for the duration of the war on the basis of the 1935 Act with some minimal scope for additional Indian representatives on the Executive Council.

On 29 March he announced the conclusions of his discussions. He proposed that:

- Dominion status would include the right of provinces not to join the Dominion
- the Executive Council should include with immediate effect an Indian as defence minister.

Cripps' proposals met with a resounding lack of approval. Cripps returned to Britain on 12 April and offered his resignation. He was persuaded to withdraw it and Parliament debated the mission's failure on 28 April.

## Failure factors

Cripps himself identified the key failure factors as the war situation, including a defeatist attitude aggravated by enemy propaganda, together with Hindu–Muslim political antagonism. More generally, the government projected the view that its generous intentions had been repudiated out of hand. This rather simplified the complicated responses, intrigues and mistakes made by the various parties.

With regard to his first task, the post-war constitution, Cripps had stuck to the British government position that when a Dominion constitution for a union of India was drawn up, provinces would be free not to join the union. Such protection of this possibility at the outset was perceived by Congress as tantamount to encouraging Muslim disengagement from Congress and India itself. Indeed, at the press conference on 29 March, Cripps discussed the possibility of two states, India and Pakistan, and even suggested altering provincial boundaries and the necessity of relocating masses of people. This was the first time a British official had publicly acknowledged this as a realistic consideration.

With regard to the second task, Cripps has been criticised for going beyond his brief. It has been suggested that, in trying to gain backing for the post-war processes, he was drawn into a proposal that the Executive Council should immediately include an Indian defence minister, which antagonised the viceroy (Linlithgow) and Churchill. The proposal was jointly made by Cripps and Colonel Louis Johnson, a personal envoy of the US president. Roosevelt had already proposed an immediate temporary Dominion government on 10 March, saying: 'Such a move is in line with the world changes of the past half-century and the democratic processes of all who are fighting Nazism.'

These interventions were greeted suspiciously by the British, who perceived them as meddlesome, since they increased resistance if anything. Linlithgow already had Churchill's support because of his hard-line approach and the war cabinet backed Linlithgow's view that the powers of the viceroy were laid out in the 1935 Act and should not be tinkered with. In truth, the fact that Linlithgow had not himself been briefed about the Cripps mission virtually ensured that he and Cripps would be at loggerheads. This lends support to the view that Churchill had always regarded the mission as a way of placating the Americans and tarnishing the reputation of Cripps, whom he might have regarded as a political rival.

## Congress rejection

Congress formally rejected the proposals on 10 April. There was little for them to support: the sole concession to them of the defence minister had been blocked, the princely states had been allowed to select rather than elect future representatives, while both the states and Muslims appeared to have gained the right to stay out of a future union of India completely. Moreover, Congress saw no point in rushing to agree if the deteriorating war situation would force the British to offer more later. Gandhi famously described the proposals as 'a post-dated cheque on a crashing bank'.

Although most observers saw Cripps as favouring Congress, Congress's rejection of the proposals again created opportunities for Muslims to bolster their position. The Muslim League accepted the proposals and was increasingly confident in challenging Congress's claim to represent all Indian opinion. Churchill, Linlithgow and Amery all saw this as a helpful weakening of Congress and an excuse to postpone matters while there was such disagreement. Churchill maintained that the British had done what they could and, indeed, US, Chinese and even Labour Party demands for progress diminished in the face of Congress's apparent ingratitude.

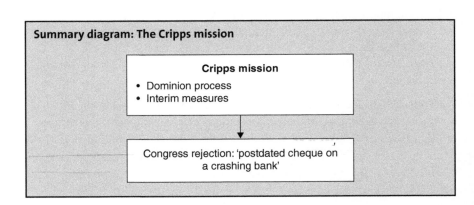

**Summary diagram: The Cripps mission**

**Cripps mission**
- Dominion process
- Interim measures

Congress rejection: 'postdated cheque on a crashing bank'

## 2 The Quit India campaign

▶ *What was the effect of suppressing the campaign?*

## Renewed civil disobedience

The failure of the Cripps mission put negotiation over constitutional reform back in the drawer **for the duration**. Accordingly, both sides saw this as the opportunity to harden their approaches still further.

Linlithgow increased press censorship while using more centralised Special Branch surveillance to intercept Congress communications. He ordered a search for information to allow him to suggest that Congress was pro-Nazi.

Gandhi declared that Britain was unable to defend India and that Indians should prepare a defence strategy of peaceful non-cooperation. He argued that, since Japan's hostility was directed at the British Empire, as soon as it was a free nation India would be able to negotiate peace with Japan. Congress declined to agree and Nehru, in particular, rejected any co-operation with a fascist power. Gandhi's response was: 'Leave India to God. If that is too much, then leave her to anarchy.'

By summer 1942 the government was aware through intercepts that a renewed campaign of civil disobedience was being planned. Linlithgow made plans to arrest the entire Congress leadership and deport them to Uganda while Gandhi would be sent to Aden, a British base in Yemen. The plan was dropped when the governor of Aden objected and a lawyer pointed out that the power of arrest would lapse on board ship.

Nevertheless, the war cabinet authorised Linlithgow to take all necessary measures after a further secret report revealed details of how the campaign would start with strikes and destruction of communications and railways. By now, the British government feared a wartime uprising. During the First World War, a rebellion by the Irish, chiefly in Dublin in 1916, had been put down but had led in 1922 to the partition of Ireland and the creation of the independent Irish Free State.

## The Quit India resolution

On 8 August 1942 the All-India Congress Committee met in Gowalia Tank park, Bombay, and its resolution is reproduced in Source B.

Gandhi declared it the moment to 'Do or die for nothing less than freedom' and called bluntly for the British to 'Quit India', which became the popular reference for the resolution.

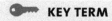

🗝 **KEY TERM**

**For the duration** Became a common phrase to describe the unknown length of the war.

*[handwritten margin note: since they were fighting w/ British empire]*

*[handwritten note above "the moment": drew up]*

? What kind of action does
the resolution in Source B
authorise?

**SOURCE B**

**Extract from the so-called 'Quit India' resolution of Congress, quoted in B.N. Pandey, editor, *The Indian Nationalist Movement 1885–1947: Select Documents*, Macmillan, 1979, p. 142.**

*… to sanction, for the vindication of India's inalienable right to freedom and independence, the starting of a mass struggle on non-violent lines on the widest possible scale … every man and woman who is participating in the movement must function for himself or herself within the four corners of the general instructions issued.*

## British response

Linlithgow ordered provincial governors to put into action prearranged plans for suppressing the civil disobedience campaign, overriding the opposition of the Executive Council. Congress leaders across India were arrested in morning raids. The Congress working committee was imprisoned in Ahmedanagar Fort near Bombay, but its members were allowed to meet freely and so continued political discussions. Gandhi was detained in the Aga Khan's palace at Poona (Pune).

Among the general population, matters were far less pleasant. The initial Delhi *hartal* resulted in arson and the killing of fourteen people by police. The leader of the Congress Socialist Party planned to seize Delhi in a guerrilla war, calling on US soldiers to support them. Unrest, arson and sabotage grew in mostly Hindu areas such as Bihar, United Provinces, Bombay and Rajputana.

In response, the police shot on sight those breaking curfew, and conducted public whippings; women were beaten with *lathis* and there were allegations of rape in custody. As violence escalated, policemen were burned to death while the British torched whole villages and used aircraft to machine-gun crowds. Hundreds were killed and about 500 arrested without trial and denied visits.

### Emergency powers

In New Delhi, the Revolutionary Movements Ordinance, a law giving the viceroy emergency powers, was implemented, struck down by the courts and reissued with dismissively slight amendments by the government. Linlithgow was determined to crack down and was oblivious to the mounting evidence that maintaining British order was more important than the British rule of law.

Meanwhile, Churchill and Linlithgow were all but competing for self-importance and self-justification. Churchill declared defiantly: 'I have not become the King's First Minister in order to preside on the liquidation of the British Empire.' Linlithgow reported to the British government:

*I am engaged here in meeting by far the most serious rebellion since that of 1857, the gravity and extent of which we have so far concealed from the world for reasons of military security. Mob violence remains rampant over large tracts of the countryside.*

Privately, he had already said that the key to success in this war was largely in his hands.

## Suppression

By the end of 1942 the British had managed to suppress the Quit India movement, using 57 infantry battalions to restore order. In the process, it was not only lives, liberties and homes which had been lost. The British had lost their moral authority within India and with US public opinion, which once again saw the British as more interested in preserving their empire than defeating the common enemies of democracy.

Matters remained tense. The Indian members of the Executive Council all resigned while Gandhi declared from his palace-prison that he would undertake a three-week fast in February 1943. Even as Gandhi's health declined, Churchill called him a 'humbug' and 'rascal', demanding that his water be checked for secret nutrition. Linlithgow announced that he would not submit to 'blackmail and terror' and made preparations for the eventuality of Gandhi's death. As a result of personal pleas, Gandhi called off his fast in March. But time was also being called on the Linlithgow era.

*↳ after backlash from Churchill + Linlithgow*

**SOURCE C**

**Public transport was a favourite target during the Quit India protests. Men and boys join together to throw stones at a tram in Calcutta, 1 April 1947.**

> Why do you think the protesters in Source C targeted public transport?

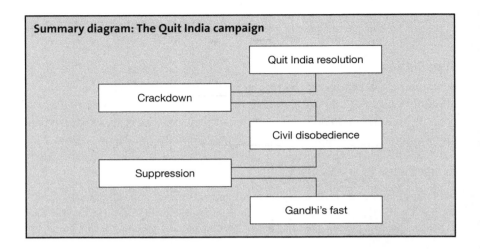

Summary diagram: The Quit India campaign

# ③ Viceroy Wavell

▶ *How did Wavell attempt to improve the political situation?*

## Wavell's appointment

Churchill had twice extended Linlithgow's term of office, largely to maintain the suppression of the Quit India civil disobedience movement. Now that was under control, there was no good reason to postpone the choice of a new viceroy. Both Leo Amery, the secretary of state for India, and Clement Attlee, the Labour Party leader (and future prime minister), were considered. In the end, however, Churchill settled on a military figure, Archibald Wavell, the commander-in-chief of India. *as new viceroy*

The choice is revealing of Churchill's priorities. At first sight, it suggested the continuation of a hard line driven by military considerations. Another view is that Wavell was considered stolid and safe, ideal for what Churchill wanted in a viceroy but not in a top general. The 'promotion' to viceroy was a useful way of putting General Claude Auchinleck in his place as commander-in-chief (in which position 'The Auk' continued in the independent Indian Army).

### The Indian situation

Wavell took over an India which was paying vast sums towards the war effort. Britain was promising to repay afterwards but the total in 1943 was already £800 million, an amount that it was inconceivable Britain could actually repay.

Amery, commenting in his diary on Churchill's stated dislike of Indians, said: 'We are getting out of India far more than was ever thought possible and … India herself is paying far more than was ever contemplated.'

**SOURCE D**

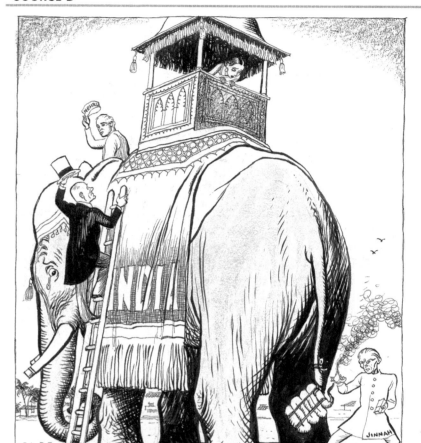

What relationship is suggested in Source D between the man on the ladder and woman (princess) by the man's outfit?

A cartoon by Leslie Illingworth, published in the *Daily Mail*, 21 August 1946, showing Viceroy Wavell's arrival in India.

Wavell, having been based in India, came to the job better prepared than most viceroys. However, he came to London to meet political leaders. He soon realised that Churchill was paying lip service to the idea of political progress in India and that he had little awareness of the situation. He commented: 'He hates India and everything to do with it and as Amery said in a note he pushed across to me: "knows as much of the Indian problem as George III did of the American colonies".' On returning to India, Wavell was told by Linlithgow that Britain would have to 'continue responsibility for India for at least another 30 years'.

Wavell became viceroy in October 1943 and, despite his experience, set about extending his knowledge and consultation. He travelled round the country, sometimes up to 1500 km per week, and convened regular meetings of the eleven provincial governors. (Linlithgow had not held one such meeting in his seven years.) Wavell worked hard for India. His military experience proved useful in two key areas during his relatively short period of office. First, his

*Overall wanted what is best for India*

response to a devastating famine in Bengal was practical and constructive. Second, he insisted on consideration of the future boundaries of India and Pakistan in order to be prepared.

## The Bengal famine

The situation in Bengal was critical. The two harvests of 1942 and 1943 had been poor, the latter the worst of the century. This was aggravated by a shortage of other foods and reduced imports because of the war and poor organisation of food distribution within the province. As a result of widespread malnutrition, people were dying more quickly of pneumonia, cholera and malaria. The death rate had risen by half as much again. In all, it is estimated that the famine caused between 1 million and 3 million deaths.

Once the famine started to affect the major cities of Dacca and Calcutta, the concern became national (even assisting recruitment to the INA). Wavell's concern was primarily humanitarian. However, Wavell no doubt realised the political danger of doing little or nothing while trying to uphold the Churchillian view that British administration was good for India. Jinnah accused the British of incompetence and contempt on the grounds that such a crisis would not have been neglected in Britain itself.

### Wavell's actions

Wavell immediately diverted soldiers from the war effort and defence of India to assist with the distribution of food. He introduced rationing and control of panic buying and profiteering. Politically, Wavell demanded the appointment of a governor for Bengal, a post which had been left vacant for no good reason. In Britain, he had to struggle against the view of Lord Cherwell, economic adviser to Churchill, that the famine was statistically improbable and with Churchill's own reluctance to spare any merchant ships to transport grain. Even the USA refused to divert any of its ships to Australia to bring in grain. However, Wavell eventually got twice what was originally promised, perhaps because it was half what he had asked for. By mid-1944, the situation was coming under control but Wavell stated to Amery that: 'The Bengal famine was one of the greatest disasters that has befallen any people under British rule and has done great damage to our reputation here.'

## Wavell's initiative

It was also clear in the summer of 1944 that the war was being won. The D-day landings had successfully launched the Allied liberation of Europe, the Soviets were throwing the Germans back on the Eastern Front and the Americans were recapturing, with more difficulty, the Pacific islands. On the borders of India, the battles of Imphal and Kohima had decisively broken the threat of Japanese invasion. With military victory in sight, it was clear that pressure would resume for discussion of the post-war political situation.

In August 1944 Wavell brought the provincial governors together for a conference to consider the political future. Some new factors could be foreseen: the war debt continued to mount as would calls for repayment to benefit India and Indians; the Indian Civil Service had been strained by the war and hundreds of thousands of soldiers, both British and Indian, would be impatient to be **demobilised** and return home. The governors were 'emphatically of the opinion' that a positive initiative should be made by the British before the end of the war. The governor of Bengal proposed the unequivocal declaration of an actual departure date.

> **KEY TERM**
>
> **Demobilised** Released from the armed forces (also called demobbed).

## British attitudes

The problem was the attitude and interference of the British government and of Churchill, in particular. The government had raised the wages of Indian soldiers without consultation with the Indian government, adding more than £50 million per year to the war debt. On the other hand, Wavell's request for an Indian finance minister on the Executive Council was rejected. All Wavell's letters to Gandhi, in prison again in India, had to be sent to London first for discussion by the war cabinet.

Far from concession, Churchill wanted to do nothing and declared that Britain was under 'no obligation to honour promises made at a time of difficulty'. While the war was on, Churchill saw the importance of keeping up morale, although that did not hinder the suppression of the Quit India movement. With peace in sight, however, there was neither the will to keep enough British soldiers in India to maintain order nor the will to supply money to create Indian forces. Indeed, ships and food were already being prioritised for the rebuilding of Europe.
↳ rather than for India

## Initiative stalled

In November 1944 Wavell requested consideration of a political initiative. For five months, the war cabinet put off responding and eventually left it to the India Committee to reject Wavell's request for any initiative. Wavell protested and was invited to London in March 1945 to make the case. He told Churchill that unrest was again growing and 'the present government of India cannot continue indefinitely or even for very long'. He declared: 'I feel very strongly that the future of India is the problem on which the British Commonwealth and the British reputation will stand or fall in the post-war period.' The trouble was that, while Churchill also saw it in terms of reputation, he was adamant that he would not go down in history as the prime minister who gave India away. The 1945 election saved him from that fate.

Wavell requested a summary of the India Committee's discussion in order to answer its concerns. The request was refused. The war cabinet stated that a precondition for progress was that Congress should officially declare the Quit India movement over. Wavell advised against stirring up what was already finished.

While Wavell was kept waiting in London for a decision, the economic adviser John Maynard Keynes presented the war cabinet with a financial analysis that showed that running the British Empire had cost £1000 million for each of the past two years, rising post-war to £1400 million per year. In sum, without US financial assistance, Britain would go bankrupt.

In the same month, April 1945, Roosevelt died. He had been a loyal but critical friend of the British when defeat had seemed possible. Now, a new president might not be so tolerant of British problems of their own making. Churchill's mind too was on managing victory parades with a view to the first general election in Britain since 1935. Almost as a way of getting Wavell out of his sight, Churchill agreed to a national conference of Indian political leaders. Wavell departed for India, commenting that it was in effect too little, too late yet again.

## The 1945 Simla Conference

Wavell moved swiftly to make the conference happen. He released the Congress working committee from prison and ignored the rejection of the initiative by the Executive Council. The new members appointed following Congress resignations could clearly see that their wartime support for the British would be swept aside by a resurgent nationalist movement.

The conference opened in **Simla** on 25 June 1945 with delegates from Congress, the Muslim League and others, both radical and loyalist. Wavell was exasperated by the assumption that votes around the table would be an acceptable way to make decisions about India's future. The conference foundered quickly on refusals and rejections in creating a new Council, although Amery accepted that the delay in agreeing to even holding a conference had stoked up resentments.

Jinnah refused to accept the legitimacy of Muslims who were not members of the Muslim League. The president of Congress was still Maulana Azad, snubbed by Jinnah as a token Muslim in a Hindu organisation. Wavell had similar concerns about Congress, but he also refused to accept that the Muslim League was the only representative organisation of Muslims.

The governors of the Punjab and of Bengal advised Wavell to set out the consequences of creating a Pakistan in order to test the true strength of Jinnah's support in these two crucial provinces with their own local Muslim leaders.

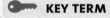

**KEY TERM**

**Simla** Pronounced Shimla, summer capital of British India, high in the cool of the mountains.

? To what extent does Wavell's view in Source E lend support to the revisionist view of Jinnah's two-nation strategy (see page 77)?

### SOURCE E

**From a letter to Secretary of State Amery from Viceroy Wavell, October 1944, quoted in B.N. Pandey, editor, *The Indian Nationalist Movement 1885–1947: Select Documents*, Macmillan, 1979, p. 157.**

*Jinnah wants Pakistan first and independence afterwards, Gandhi wants independence first with some kind of self-determination for Muslims to be granted by a provisional government which would be predominantly Hindu. It is difficult to believe that Jinnah who, whatever his faults, is a highly intelligent man, is sincere about the 'two nations' theory. His refusal to answer awkward*

*questions also shows that he has not thought out the implications of Pakistan,
or anyway will not disclose his views on them. To take only one example, the
north-eastern Muslim state would amount to very little without Calcutta, but
Calcutta is in the main a Hindu city. On the other hand, Jinnah's suspicion of
Gandhi is justified. Gandhi's ideal, though he is careful not to express it, is a
unified India in which the Hindus, given a free rein, would inevitably dominate
the Muslims. Jinnah was arguing for something which he has not worked out
fully, and Gandhi was putting forward counter-proposals in which he did not
really believe at all.*

Instead, Wavell proposed an Interim Council, with a membership list drawn
up by himself. This was rejected by Jinnah, who sensed his growing popular
strength with every refusal to compromise.

The conference broke up and shortly afterwards the political landscape was itself
shattered. In July 1945 the British electorate voted unsentimentally to throw
out Churchill, the great wartime leader, in favour of the socialist Attlee at the
head of a Labour government committed to radical social reform. The omens for
Indian nationalism had never looked better.

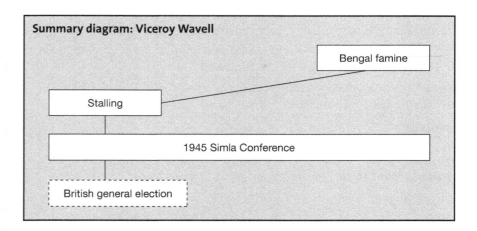

**Summary diagram: Viceroy Wavell**

- Bengal famine
- Stalling
- 1945 Simla Conference
- British general election

# 4 Attempts at political settlement 1945–6

▶ *To what extent did the new Labour government change Indian
politics?*

## The Labour government's Indian policy

The new Labour government was determined to press ahead with political
reform in India and there was optimism among nationalist leaders that progress

towards independence would quicken. The two main aims were to revive democratic politics by holding elections for the eleven British provincial councils and the central assemblies and to form an (unelected) group to start work on a new constitution.

There was some concern among the British in India that the British government was not sufficiently aware of the scale of support for the Pakistan movement and that elections would provide a huge boost to the campaign. Nehru had said that he would not work with the Muslim League while Jinnah was strengthening the demand for Pakistan.

## Fear of unrest

Viceroy Wavell was worried that Labour was too eager to hand over power to Congress, which would further raise the anxieties of the Muslim League. He was acutely aware of the potential for unrest – from food and coal shortages as much as anything – and the weakness of the British situation if the revival of politics led to renewed civil disobedience.

At the end of the war in August 1945 there were about 50,000 soldiers available in India (that is, just one for every 8000 civilians) but, tired after the war, they were eager to be demobbed and return to their homes, whether Indian or British. There was no possibility that extra troops would be sent. Moreover, any state of emergency would itself be more serious than ever before because of the widespread availability of unreturned weapons.

Wavell wrote to the new secretary of state for India, Freddie Pethick-Lawrence, in November 1945 (see Source F).

### SOURCE F

**From a letter from Viceroy Wavell to the secretary of state, documented in *Transfer of Power*, volume VI, p. 451, quoted in P. French, *Liberty or Death*, Flamingo, 1997, p. 217.**

*We are now faced in India with a situation of great difficulty and danger ... I must warn His Majesty's Government to be prepared for a serious attempt by the Congress, probably next spring, but quite possibly earlier to subvert by force the present administration in India ... the choice will lie between capitulating to Congress and accepting their demands and using all our resources to suppress the movement.*

? What is Wavell's assessment of the danger in Source F?

## Courts martial and mutinies

The British did not help the situation by their handling of the defeated INA. It became clear that Indians generally supported the captured soldiers. Congress called for their release, declaring that they had worked, however misguidedly, for the freedom of India.

The British officer class nevertheless still wanted to make the point that the INA were traitors and court-martialled a sample of three senior officers, deliberately choosing a Hindu, a Muslim and a Sikh. This simply united the three communities and their leaders in opposition. The officers were convicted of waging war against the Crown, a charge carrying a potential death penalty. They were actually sentenced to transportation for life, but then this was abandoned and they were released in case the general mood in the Indian Army turned angry.

There were mutinies in February 1946 (and indeed there was unrest among British troops unhappy about the slow pace of demobilisation). A total of 20,000 sailors from the Royal Indian Navy in Bombay, then Calcutta and Karachi, took over nearly 80 ships and a general strike was called by the Bombay Communist Party. However, Congress leaders persuaded the mutineers to surrender. This angered many supporters but the leadership of both Congress and the Muslim League saw more advantage for the moment in co-operating with the British than in resistance.

## The Indian elections

It was clear to nationalist leaders that the British were now serious about quitting India, which meant gauging the strength of the demand for Pakistan. In January 1946 a small fact-finding visit by British MPs came and went without announcing their conclusions but, in private, some stated that Pakistan must be conceded to avoid Muslim unrest. Work began secretly on deciding how the country could be partitioned. Viceroy Wavell was keenly interested in making practical preparations for the eventual unpleasantness of announcing the actual boundary lines. It was immediately apparent that the Punjab would be a flashpoint split between a Muslim-west and Hindu-east but with 5 million Sikhs spread throughout. The Sikh holy city of Amritsar was surrounded by a Muslim-majority area, potentially cut off in a future Pakistan. Meanwhile, British and Indian politicians were waiting to see how the land lay after the Indian general election in the spring of 1946.

The message of the 1946 election results in the eleven British provinces was even greater polarisation of support:

- Congress won a convincing victory with 90 per cent of seats overall, and formed provincial governments in eight provinces.
- The Muslim League won 75 per cent of all Muslim votes, and took 90 per cent of the seats reserved for Muslims in the provinces and all 30 Muslim seats in the central assembly. It formed two rather shaky provincial governments in Bengal and Sind (see below).
- A non-Muslim coalition took power in the Punjab, even though the Muslim League had the largest number of votes and took 75 of the 88 Muslim seats.
- Congress was shocked to realise that it would have to face up to the Muslim League and their Pakistan campaign.
- However, Muslims had voted most strongly for the League in Muslim-minority provinces that could never realistically be part of Pakistan. They

appeared to support the idea of a separate Muslim state as a haven to which they might move.

- In the areas which were already Muslim-majority, there appeared to be more interest and confidence in maintaining local power. In Bengal, for example, Huseyn Shaheed Suhrawardy, the local Muslim League leader, tried to form a regional coalition with Congress in order to campaign for a united, and possibly independent, Bengal. In Sind province, the local Muslim League broke away from the national organisation with the aim of autonomy: an independent mini-Pakistan.
- In the North West Frontier Province, the Pathan tribes, although Muslim, were loyal to their leader, who was against the League and the idea of Pakistan. Accordingly, Congress held power in this far-flung area.

## The cabinet mission

In order to push forward with Labour's second aim – the drafting of a new constitution – Prime Minister Clement Attlee gained cabinet agreement for another mission to India. It was widely expected that this new peacetime mission, from a socialist government which clearly intended to honour promises of independence, would be successful. The formal brief was to consult about setting up a process whereby Indian independence could be 'determined by Indians with the minimum of disturbance and the maximum of speed'. The confidential brief was not just to listen but to create positive desire for a speedy transfer of power. However, in the words of Woodrow Wyatt, a Labour MP: 'they tried to give away an Empire but found their every suggestion for doing it frustrated by the intended recipients'.

The mission, including eleven civil servants, was nominally headed by the secretary of state, Pethick-Lawrence, but actually driven by Cripps, now president of the board of trade in the cabinet, seeking to reverse the embarrassing failure of his 1942 mission. The third man was A.V. Alexander, first lord of the admiralty but actually a very traditional Labour politician.

The mission met Indian politicians on 1 April 1946 and invited the various leaders to state their demands or aspirations. Gandhi argued defiantly that the power to make decisions about and for India should be transferred to Congress, as it was the election winner. Jinnah recognised that there was no hope of an independent, Congress-dominated India agreeing to Pakistan. It could only come into existence from a British decision. The British needed Muslim co-operation in order to avoid disorder and present an agreed peaceful transfer to the world. So Jinnah avoided confrontation and waited. Gandhi made a wily suggestion that Jinnah form a government balanced by a Hindu majority in the central assembly, prompting Wavell to observe that 'he is a tough politician and not a saint'.

Meanwhile, there was no Sikh representative and little attention paid to this vulnerable minority. Similarly, the position of the princely states was ignored.

**SOURCE G**

'**Three innocents in the jungle of India/Pakistan**', a cartoon by Leslie Illingsworth, published in the *Daily Mail*, **25 February 1946.**

> What does Source G suggest about the likely success of the cabinet mission?

The princes had treaties with Britain which could not force them to become part of an independent India. In theory, they had the right to remain as autonomous petty states scattered across India.

The behaviour of the British delegation was counter-productive. Pethick-Lawrence wanted Indian independence so much that he left the British no bargaining power. He tended to agree with every demand, earning him the secret nickname 'Pathetic Lawrence'. Cripps, meanwhile, enjoyed holding secret meetings but then made no secret of his closeness to Gandhi.

## The 1946 Simla Conference

In May 1946 Indian political leaders were invited to Simla for a conference to discuss the two constitutional options drawn up by the cabinet mission and approved by the full British cabinet. Wavell joined the three-man delegation to form the British party with four representatives each from Congress and the Muslim League.

The mood was not good. Jinnah refused to speak to Maulana Azad, one of the two Muslim Congress representatives. Gandhi, although not formally involved, turned up on a special train to announce that he would block any moves towards partition.

The first, preferred option attempted to be imaginative and flexible. It proposed a single state with a three-tier constitutional structure:

*1st option*

- a minimal 'union government', responsible for foreign affairs, defence and communication
- self-selected regional *groupings* of provinces exercising all other governmental powers
- the existing provinces.

More controversially, it was proposed that the regional groupings might be permitted after a period of time to secede from the original union by means of **plebiscites** to become independent states. The second, fall-back option was the first formal proposal of a two-state outcome: **Hindustan** and Pakistan. The *2nd* two states would conclude formal treaties with each other but would have no common government.

The hope was that Congress would recoil from the second option and support the first. It had the attraction of producing a Congress-dominated single state but they would have to accept the right of provincial groupings to secede. On the other side, although the Muslim League would obviously prefer the second option, they might be persuaded to accept the first if they were confident that sustained demand for Pakistan would allow it to emerge democratically.

The British cabinet was concerned about the viability of a Pakistani state in itself as well as the effect of splitting the Indian armed forces. There is, however, some evidence that the British regarded a future Pakistan as more loyal to British strategic interests in central Asia than a future India (see page 132).

In the end, perhaps predictably, Congress could not give its support to either option since they could both lead, sooner or later, to partition. After two full sessions of the conference, with no prospect of agreement, Pethick-Lawrence wound up proceedings.

With hindsight, historians have speculated about the role of the failing health of Jinnah. Jinnah's public stance of waiting until people came round to the idea of Pakistan was at odds with his personal fear that he did not have long to live. He wanted to see Pakistan born before he died and he wanted to be its first leader. He could not afford to wait another ten years or more for plebiscites to take place.

*he was ill*

If Congress and the British had known how seriously ill he was, they might have been tempted to slow down and wait for him to die in the hope that the momentum would go out of the Pakistan movement. It is one of the great 'might have been' questions of the period.

## SOURCE H

**From an article in the Lahore *Tribune* newspaper by Sheikh Abdullah, president of the Kashmir National Conference, 9 January 1946, quoted in B.N. Pandey, editor, *The Indian Nationalist Movement 1885–1947: Select Documents*, Macmillan, 1979, p. 184.**

*Pakistan will rescue Muslims from Hindu domination. This is the current popular argument; on the face of it this argument appeals, Muslims being in the position of a minority. But there are provinces in India where Muslims are in the majority. Obviously they do not need Pakistan. If it is needed at all it is needed by Muslims in the Muslim minority provinces … . It is they who need to be rescued from the domination of Hindus. Yet it is they who are being kept out of the orbit of Pakistan. This is undoubtedly a curious solution and unjust.*

*Secondly, in spite of notions of Muslims being one and a cultural community, provincial animosities between the different units of Pakistan are bound to come to the forefront sooner than later. … because of these hatreds and animosities which are more deep-rooted than all the current cant about religious affinity the different units of the proposed Pakistan would find it hard to be bossed over by one another and they may as a result demand some kind of a near self-determination.*

## SOURCE I

**From a note by Jawaharlal Nehru, 10 July 1946, *Indian Annual Register 1946*, volume 2, pp. 145–7, quoted in B.N. Pandey, editor, *The Indian Nationalist Movement 1885–1947: Select Documents*, Macmillan, 1979, p. 197.**

*The big probability is that from any approach to the question there will be no grouping. Obviously Section A (Sind, Punjab, North West Frontier Province) will decide against grouping. Speaking in betting language there was 4 to 1 chance [sic] of the North West Frontier Province deciding against grouping. Then Group B (Assam, Bengal) collapses. It is highly likely that Assam will decide against grouping with Bengal, although I would not like to say what the initial decision may be, since it is evenly balanced. But I can say with every assurance and conviction that there is going to be finally no grouping there, because Assam will not tolerate it under any circumstances whatever. Thus you see this grouping business approached from a point of view does not get on at all.*

> ? Summarise the positions shown in Sources H and I of these two leaders, one Muslim, one Congress, with regard to the viability of regional groupings of provinces.

## The May statement

Having failed to reach agreement in the Simla conferences, the cabinet mission moved matters on by making a declaration of intent, leaving it up to the

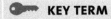

**KEY TERM**

**Constituent assembly**
A parliament with the sole task of designing a constitution.

various Indian parties to agree or not. They announced that they would create a **constituent assembly** of elected representatives from the eleven British provinces. The assembly would draft a constitution for the single state with regional groupings.

Congress declined to accept the May statement. However, on 6 June the Muslim League did accept it and Jinnah spoke publicly to emphasise the personal compromise he had made in accepting the right of a constituent assembly to decide about Pakistan.

The cabinet mission further announced that it would create an interim government composed entirely of Indians, with the exception of Wavell as governor-general. However, this plan got stuck on the proportions of members for different communities. Jinnah insisted on choosing all the Muslim representatives, while Congress insisted on being able to choose Muslims for the Congress section. A Sikh and a Christian representative were added, followed by a Dalit and then a Parsi.

*M+H not decided*

As time moved on, a further (June) statement announced that the viceroy would select members for any group which did not immediately accept the May statement.

## Congress counter-interpretation

On 24 June Congress suddenly announced a partial acceptance of the May statement. They were clearly seeking to avoid being excluded but they also proposed a counter-interpretation of the groupings plan. They argued that if groupings could secede from the nation-state, then individual provinces could opt out of regional groupings, either to become autonomous or merge back into the (Indian) state. Their hope was, of course, that this would fragment Pakistan if it ever got formed. To the anger of Wavell and Jinnah, Cripps declined to rule out this interpretation.

On 27 June Jinnah, feeling betrayed, announced that constitutional methods had failed. The cabinet mission left India and Wavell wrote: 'The Mission gave away the weakness of our position and our bluff has been called. Our time in India is limited and our power to control events almost gone.'

Wavell announced the imminent formation of the interim government on the basis of six Congress nominees, five from the Muslim League and three chosen by Wavell to represent minorities. When the Muslim League declined to nominate anyone, Wavell agreed that Congress should choose additional Muslim representatives. The Muslim League responded by withdrawing its previous agreement to the May statement and instructed all Muslim officials to resign.

## Withdrawal plans

As the political process broke down, so the country slid towards civil war. The commander-in-chief, Auchinleck, warned on 13 August that 'in the event of civil war, the Indian armed forces cannot be relied on'. Wavell was advised to 'leave India to her fate'. He wanted to announce a phased withdrawal which would be completed by 1 January 1947, just five months later. However, the British government wanted no sense of panic so Wavell was refused troop reinforcements. He had almost been refused permission to even make plans for the evacuation of 100,000 European civilians, including many families, and only just got promises of extra ships if necessary.

Then, in the heat of August 1946, Jinnah made a great misjudgement.

## The Great Calcutta Killings

Jinnah had decided that the time had come to show that the Muslim League could also use direct mass action like Gandhi and Congress. Jinnah had so far deplored the use of such action, regarding it as a form of intimidation, and preferred entirely peaceful means of constitutional negotiation. However, he now despaired of negotiations because of the tactics and behaviour of Congress leaders and was confident of a show of strength because of the election results. This combination of inexperience, confidence and despair perhaps led him to underestimate the forces he was about to unleash.

Jinnah called for a 'universal Muslim *hartal*' on 16 August 1946, which was declared Direct Action Day. The symbolic focus of the strike was a huge Muslim League procession through Calcutta. Jinnah's intention was entirely peaceful and League leaders had persuaded the relatively new British governor of Bengal, Sir Frederick Burrows, to declare a public holiday, with the result that the army was withdrawn to barracks.

The tens of thousands of marching Muslims had provided themselves with *lathis* and rocks, for either self-defence or aggression. Hindus threw stones as they passed. At the final mass rally of 100,000 marchers, the chief minister of Bengal, H.S. Suhrawardy, is thought to have incited violence against local Hindus. As darkness fell, the crowd moved off and the attacks began in the slums and the docks. There followed three days and nights of rioting, lynching, killing and arson before troops gained control again. Hundreds of bodies were left in the streets. The toll is now thought to have been 6000 people dead, nearly 20,000 wounded and 100,000 made homeless. Most of the latter moved to areas already strong in numbers of their religious community – a portent of the desperate migrations to come (see page 127).

### Causes and consequences

Congress held the governor responsible for failing to prepare for rioting. However, elsewhere in India, the *hartal* caused no trouble at all. It was assumed that, since Muslims were responsible for the march, the vast majority of victims were Hindu. This is not now thought to be the case. Commentators now believe that the initial trouble was exploited by the many underworld gangs of the vast, poor city of Calcutta, looking to settle scores and indulge in looting.

The outcome of the Calcutta massacres was the destruction of any optimism that the communities and their leaders might offer compromises. The slope towards partition along communal lines had tipped steeply. For Jinnah, it was a personal catastrophe. His reputation for wise leadership was damaged, whether one believed that he knew what he was doing or that the Muslim League could not manage its own community discipline.

Congress, notwithstanding its numerical strength, now felt the injured party and resorted to working outside and against negotiations. Gandhi warned Wavell that Congress would not try to calm any future trouble if that actually meant using British troops as a back-up. Behind the scenes, Gandhi instructed the Congress representative in London to try to set up a secret meeting with the prime minister. Attlee agreed not only to the meeting but also to the suggestion that Wavell should be replaced as viceroy. Wavell became aware of this and, despite (false) reassurances from Attlee, it was clear that Congress was succeeding in undermining him.

## The interim government

The long-awaited interim government took power on 2 September 1946, a moment described by the historian Patrick French as more important than independence nearly a year later. The 1935 Act had shifted power at the provincial level; now the balance of power at the national level shifted over to nationalist politicians.

The viceroy was still responsible for the effective government of British India and relations with the princely states. However, as governor-general in council, the same person was now obliged to carry out the decisions of Indian ministers and members of Executive Council. Since the Muslim League had withdrawn its representatives, this meant that Congress was now in charge of India, including foreign affairs, which were the personal responsibility of Nehru as vice-president of the Executive Council. Congress general secretary, Sardar Patel, was responsible for **home affairs**, which included security and the secret services. He immediately diverted the flow of intelligence reports to the Congress administration, cutting out the viceroy.

Wavell persevered with attempts to bring the Muslim League back into the interim government and in October it agreed to join the Executive Council. However, it was clear that it was not from a position of strength. The League did not have a veto over legislation concerning Muslims as it had previously demanded. Jinnah declined to join the Executive Council because of Nehru's dominance and appointed Liaquat Ali Khan in his place. When Wavell proposed the Muslim League be responsible for home affairs, Congress threatened to bring down the new government and Jinnah, avoiding a trial of strength, agreed to become finance minister.

To complicate matters still further, relations between Nehru and Patel had broken down since the elections for Congress president in April 1946. Patel had secured the votes of twelve of the fifteen provincial Congress committees, but Gandhi made it clear he wanted Nehru and so it was decided.

## Breakdown plan

Murderous consequences of the Calcutta killings spread throughout the final months of 1946. Muslims in Bihar province were killed in retaliation for the killing of Hindus in east Bengal, who had themselves been killed in reprisal for the Calcutta violence. There was almost continuous rioting in Bengal, Bombay, Bihar and the United Provinces. The terror included forced conversions to Islam and forced marriages to Muslims. At Meerut, a police officer's wife was murdered with her eight children. Whole villages were destroyed and areas cleared of one community or the other. Twenty thousand Bihari Muslims died in 1947, with tens of thousands on the move.

In November, Wavell again warned the secretary of state, Pethick-Lawrence, that the country was on the brink of civil war and asked for guidance. Auchinleck, the commander-in-chief of the Indian Army, agreed that the situation would require a military retreat. They prepared a secret breakdown plan. In the event of the collapse of the interim government and law and order, all British civilians and families would be moved speedily to heavily protected safe zones near the coast in the north-east and west. They would be evacuated from Karachi and Calcutta. British troops would also be withdrawn, leaving only Indian forces to maintain any order. Attlee refused to agree to the plan, saying that it would be accepting defeat. In fact, Attlee was stalling while he considered replacing Wavell, a situation which only let matters get worse.

## The London talks

Eventually, Attlee agreed to summon Indian leaders to talks in London. Nehru, Jinnah, Liaquat Ali Khan and Balder Singh for the Sikhs engaged in four days of talks with Wavell and Attlee. The Muslim League was continuing to insist on the basic interpretation of the May statement, namely that groupings of provinces could secede from an independent India. On this basis, they saw no need for a further constituent assembly.

British constitutional experts agreed with this interpretation, but Attlee had taken against the Muslim League, describing Jinnah as 'an Indian fascist'. He reassured Nehru of his support for Congress. They would press ahead with the constituent assembly and Nehru flew back for its opening. Jinnah remained at his residence in London, laid low by illness and disappointment. The 79 Muslim seats in the constituent assembly would be boycotted so there was no urgency to return.

Wavell, too, stayed on to press the case for a retreat plan. He also wanted decisions about the employment or pensions of the tens of thousands of British officials about to become unemployed upon independence. He made no progress. Indeed, his position was further weakened by the British appointment of a high commissioner to handle relations between the Indian interim government and the British government, leaving the viceroy a figurehead.

## Constituent assembly

The constituent assembly convened on 7 December 1946 but would never complete its task. Muslim demands for separate states grew ever stronger. Attlee was privately determined to force the issue by replacing Wavell with a new viceroy eager to hand over power as soon as possible.

In February 1947 Wavell was recalled to London and told it was time for a change at the top. He was offered an earldom but no thanks for his work as viceroy. He was in effect sacked without dignity and everyone knew it. His view was that the Attlee government seemed as unclear what to do as Churchill's wartime government had been clear what not to do.

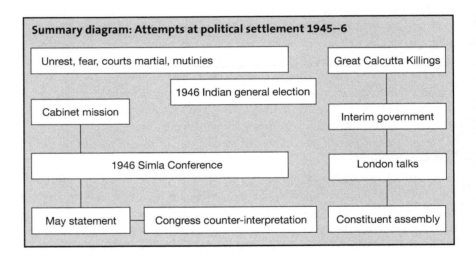

**Summary diagram: Attempts at political settlement 1945–6**

- Unrest, fear, courts martial, mutinies
- Great Calcutta Killings
- 1946 Indian general election
- Cabinet mission
- Interim government
- 1946 Simla Conference
- London talks
- May statement
- Congress counter-interpretation
- Constituent assembly

## Chapter summary

Churchill was under pressure from several forces. The Japanese enemy was advancing towards India's borders, the Indian nationalists saw no reason to give up their demands and the Americans supported their cause. Churchill dispatched Cripps to persuade Indians of British commitment to some form of change after the war. However, Cripps made recommendations unacceptable to Parliament. In response, Congress launched its most robust campaign so far, calling on the British to Quit India. Viceroy Linlithgow suppressed the protests but was replaced by Lord Wavell, a military commander more practical than political. Wavell laid plans for the safe withdrawal of the British from India, including secret plans at this stage for possible partition.

The Allied victory and landslide general election victories for Labour in Britain and Congress in India quickened hopes of rapid movement towards independence. The Labour cabinet sent another mission to discuss a new Indian constitution but relations between the nationalist parties were increasingly hostile, and an uncharacteristic call from Jinnah for street protests turned into running massacres in Calcutta. However, an interim Indian government came into existence with real practical power for the first time. A constituent assembly was convened but Wavell continued to make plans assuming the worst case.

 ## Refresher questions

Use these questions to remind yourself of the key material covered in this chapter.

1 What was the USA's attitude to Britain's problems with India?

2 Why did the Cripps mission fail?

3 What were the consequences of the Quit India resolution?

4 What problems did Wavell face at the 1945 Simla Conference?

5 How did the end of the war affect the position of the British?

6 What were the outcomes of the 1946 Indian general election?

7 What did the cabinet mission achieve?

8 What proposals were crystallised at the 1946 Simla Conference?

9 What did the May statement propose?

10 What were the consequences of Jinnah's day of action?

11 What was the significance of the interim government?

12 What was the breakdown plan?

#  Question practice

## ESSAY QUESTIONS

1  To what extent was the British government responsible for the failure of the Cripps mission?

2  The cabinet mission 'tried to give away an empire but found their every suggestion for doing it frustrated by the intended recipients'. How far do you agree with this statement?

3  To what extent did Churchill's views accelerate the decolonisation of India?

4  How significant (to the outcome of independence negotiations) was Jinnah's determination that the Muslim League be recognised as the sole voice protecting the position of Muslims?

## SOURCE ANALYSIS QUESTIONS

1  Why is Source E (page 94) valuable to the historian for an enquiry into a change in Jinnah's strategy, between 1942 and 1947, for achieving protection of Muslim political representation? Explain your answer using the source, the information given about it and your own knowledge of the historical context.

2  How much weight do you give the evidence of Source A (page 84) for an enquiry into the Churchill's and Roosevelt's understanding of the aim of the war, and any strategy for defending India? Explain your answer using the source, the information given about it and your own knowledge of the historical context.

3  How far could the historian make use of Sources H and I (page 101) together to investigate the failure of the cabinet mission in 1946? Explain your answer using the sources, the information given about them and your own knowledge of the historical context.

## CHAPTER 6

# Withdrawal, partition and independence 1947–8

In March 1947 Lord Mountbatten was appointed the final viceroy of India, with instructions to transfer power by 30 June 1948. However, relations between Congress and the Muslim League were breaking down so badly that this was not easy to accomplish. Although many had assumed that the borders between India and Pakistan were a formality, once independence arrived, it suddenly mattered enormously to people which side they were on. Terrible massacres took place among those trying to get across the border. The largest peacetime transfer of power in history ended in conflict and bloodshed.

This chapter examines:

★ Mountbatten and the partition plan

★ Partition and independence

★ British withdrawal and communal violence

The key debate on *page 135* asks the question: A shameful flight? Did the British rush the final transfer of power?

## Key dates

| | | | | | |
|---|---|---|---|---|---|
| 1947 | March 22 | Mountbatten became the final viceroy | July 4 | | Independence of India Act |
| | March | Congress accepted Pakistan demand | July 8 | | Territorial partition work began |
| | May 3 | Plan Balkan | July 19 | | Interim government split |
| | May 10 | Mountbatten showed Nehru Plan Balkan at Simla | Aug. 14/15 | | India's independence at midnight |
| 1947 | June 3 | Announcement of final plan for independence and partition | | 1948 | Deaths of Gandhi and Jinnah |

## 1 Mountbatten and the partition plan

▶ *How did Viceroy Mountbatten plan for the British handover?*

## The appointment of Mountbatten

Attlee's choice of Lord Louis Mountbatten as the new viceroy was highly appropriate. Mountbatten was a military commander in the region and

# Lord Louis Mountbatten

| | |
|---|---|
| 1900 | Born |
| 1942 | Dieppe Raid |
| 1943 | Supreme Allied commander, South East Asia |
| 1947 | Last viceroy of India |
| 1947–8 | First governor-general of independent India |
| 1979 | Died in a bomb attack |

Louis (Dickie) Mountbatten was born into a branch of the British royal family and was the great-uncle of Prince Charles. He served in the Royal Navy in the First and Second World Wars, during which he planned the disastrous Dieppe Raid (1942).

His was an enthusiast for technical innovations, some of which, such as a device to maintain safe distance between ships, became standard throughout the navy while others, such as an aircraft carrier made from reinforced ice, had to be blocked. He rose to become supreme commander in South East Asia, based in Ceylon (now Sri Lanka), although risky military adventures had to be restrained by advisers and Churchill. He regarded his appointment as viceroy (for what would clearly be a short space of time) as

an interruption of his naval career. He was later first sea lord and chief of the general staff, becoming the longest serving officer in the armed forces.

According to historian Lawrence James, 'Opinion is divided over his talents as a naval commander, strategic planner and as viceroy. He believed he had succeeded in all these undertakings in an exemplary manner and said so frequently.'

Mountbatten described himself as 'the most conceited person I know'. Attlee described him as 'rather a **Ruritanian** figure'. Mountbatten cheerfully admitted that both he and his wife had affairs. He openly encouraged intimacy between Lady Edwina and Nehru, widely thought by contemporary politicians, but never proven, to be an affair. According to James, 'What was in every sense a trivial affair added to Muslim fears that her husband was in Congress' pocket.'

Lord Mountbatten was killed by the Provisional Irish Republican Army, which exploded a bomb aboard his fishing yacht in Ireland in 1979.

 **KEY TERMS**

**Ruritanian** From an imaginary place of intrigue and romance.

**Plenipotentiary powers** The capacity to make decisions without approval from government.

known privately to be sympathetic to the Labour government. With his royal connections (he was the King's cousin), it suggested that the British would be leaving India with dignity and high ceremony.

It is generally accepted that Mountbatten was full of self-importance, unjustified by his war record, for example. He claimed that he had successfully demanded **plenipotentiary powers** and was the first viceroy to appoint a press attaché and film crew to publicise his actions. Historian Stanley Wolpert states that Mountbatten knew the viceroyalty would be an interruption, however grand, to his naval career and he was determined to be brisk in handing India back. (The Admiralty Fleet Orders officially referred to him as 'seconded temporary duty Viceroy'). Attlee's choice of the young Earl of Listowel to replace Pethick-Lawrence as secretary of state indicated that no one of great experience would be available to counterbalance Mountbatten's enthusiasm.

In contrast to the public display of power and self-confidence, Mountbatten also insisted privately on clear instructions from the Attlee government about political objectives. He wanted no setbacks to this final glorious viceroyalty. The instructions Mountbatten received were to complete the transfer of power no later than the end of June 1948, having concluded a fair deal for the princely states and preserved the united strength of the Indian Army. The public announcement of his appointment on 18 March 1947 included the objective of obtaining a unitary government for British India and the Indian (princely) states, if possible within the British Commonwealth. This latter point was Attlee's, and the King's, last main hope.

## The work of Mountbatten

Mountbatten took over on 22 March. In later recollection, he claimed: 'I realised I had been made into the most powerful man on earth. One fifth of humanity I held in my hand. A power of life and death.' In reality, political events had a growing momentum of their own and Mountbatten needed to win approvals from politicians just as before. Patel saw it immediately and remarked that Mountbatten was a toy for Nehru to play with.

**SOURCE A**

> What does Source A suggest about the relationship between the Mountbattens and Nehru? **?**

**Nehru (third from left), with Lady Mountbatten to his right and Lord Mountbatten (far right), photographed in 1947.**

Mountbatten engaged in a series of meetings with political leaders while his wife, Lady Edwina, accompanied him in uniform on visits to troubled areas. Mountbatten was charmed by Congress politicians. Nehru, with his English public school education, was a favourite and was given time to be privately spiteful about Jinnah, whom Mountbatten indiscreetly referred to as 'an evil genius … a psychopathic case'. Mountbatten admired Patel's bluntness but Dr Ambedkar (see page 61) insisted to him that Congress did not represent the 60 million Dalits (nor the 3 million Christians).

### Political stakes

The political stakes were higher than ever. The British wanted a peaceful handover under international scrutiny. The Muslims found Mountbatten much less sympathetic than Wavell but knew that the best hope for Pakistan still lay with a British reluctance to simply walk away from a political disaster. For its part, the Congress leadership had come to the view that the first cabinet mission proposal – for a federal state – would actually weaken the control of the national organisation.

Accordingly, and rather suddenly, in March 1947 Patel and Nehru persuaded the Congress working committee to accept publicly the demand for Pakistan (provided half the Punjab remained in India) in order to avoid accepting regional power blocks. The Congress leadership had decided that even if Pakistan came into existence, it could not survive economically or politically and it would be reabsorbed back into a strongly centralised state of India. Such a victory would be worth both the gamble and the wait.

### April conference

In April 1947 Mountbatten convened a conference of the eleven British provincial governors. They expressed grave concerns about the continuing growth of unrest and the likelihood of civil war given the increasing numbers of armed groups 'defending' the political parties. They recommended the earliest possible announcement of a definite plan for independence and partition if necessary.

It was also clear to all that no plan had a chance of peace without the agreement of Congress. Mountbatten thought that only a 'clean partition' would satisfy them. This would be no easy matter since Jinnah was now arguing that the two potential halves of Pakistan, east and west, should be linked by a land corridor, hundreds of kilometres in length, cutting through Indian territory but presumably under Pakistani control.

## The partition plan

### Plan Balkan

Mountbatten's first plan for an independent future was presented in secret to the British cabinet on 3 May. It has become known as Plan Balkan after the European region renowned for splintered states almost continually at war.

The plan proposed that all decisions would be freely made at the provincial level. So, the eleven British provinces would be allowed to decide whether to be autonomous or join to form larger groups, not necessarily of comparable size. The provinces of Bengal and Punjab would be able to partition themselves if that was the popular preference. The princely states could also remain individually autonomous or join with others including former British provinces.

At best, this might be seen to permit or secure local agreement in the hope of a process of gradual formation of economically stronger groups. At worst, it seemed that Mountbatten was trying to wash his hands of any decision-making from the start. The cabinet was not impressed but made only minor amendments such as confirming that the North West Frontier Province could become independent from a Pakistan almost all around it. Mountbatten announced that he would reveal the plan at a conference of Indian leaders to be held before the end of May.

Meanwhile, Patel was calling for the immediate transfer of power to let Indians make their own plans, while the most high-ranking Indian in the Indian Army declared that a military dictatorship was probably the best course of action.

## The Simla moment

Before the momentous announcement, Mountbatten took a private break with his wife at the viceregal summer residence in Simla. They were joined, at the viceroy's request, by Nehru and his daughter, Indira. Whatever the truth about the personal relationships of the Mountbattens with Nehru, it certainly risked accusations of political favouritism to invite Nehru at this sensitive time. But perhaps Mountbatten planned to use social appearances to cover a political move which was clearly unfair and would have been indefensible if it had become public. This move was to check with Nehru first that he was happy with the plan.

During the night of 10 May Mountbatten showed Nehru the short document setting out his plan (Balkan) and asked him to give his response in the morning. Some consider this to have been a sign of his growing nervousness about the plan. Perhaps Mountbatten hoped that before the plan became public he could alter any matters likely to make Congress object. If that was his thought, he had a rude awakening.

Nehru sent him a confidential note on the morning of 11 May which slashed the plan. Nehru called it 'a picture of fragmentation, conflict and disorder', which would create a multitude of **Ulsters** all over the continent. Nehru blamed the British government for the impracticality and unacceptability of the plan, but that was perhaps to avoid embarrassing Mountbatten. Nevertheless, one of Mountbatten's team said that not only was: 'British policy … once more in ruins but [Mountbatten] had endured a personal and most humiliating rebuff.'

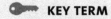

**KEY TERM**

**Ulster** Province in the north of Ireland which chose to remain fully British in 1922 when the Irish Free State was created as a Dominion.

Mountbatten asserted at a crisis meeting with his advisers on 11 May that the plan had only contained what Indians had previously indicated they would agree to and that his midnight tryst with Nehru had at any rate saved the day.

## The Menon (3 June) Plan

In public, there was no immediate change to the intention of announcing the plan on 20 May. Behind the scenes, of course, an entirely new plan had to be decided and approved by the British cabinet. Moreover, by seeking Nehru's secret approval once already, Mountbatten had effectively committed himself to ensuring his prior approval for any back-up plan. According to historian Lawrence James, 'There was a strong element of panic in Mountbatten's dash to fabricate a second plan that would satisfy Congress.'

With only hours before Nehru was due to leave Simla, V.P. Menon, the Indian reforms commissioner, was asked by Mountbatten to turn the dormant second cabinet mission plan into a credible document. This he did. Nehru pronounced himself satisfied. This two or three hours' work became the basis for the greatest peacetime transfer of power in history.

The Menon Plan stated the following:

- Two states, India and Pakistan, with Dominion status in what was now called the Commonwealth, would be created. The states would use the existing political structures of the 1935 Act until they wished to alter them (according to their different wishes).
- Provincial assemblies would decide which state to join, with the Bengal and Punjab assemblies also voting on the question of provincial partitions.
- The princes would decide whether to join either India or Pakistan as states or, as before, insist on their autonomy.

Mountbatten informed the cabinet that the plan they had approved was now dead in the water but he had another. He was summoned to London with Menon and the original date for announcement of the plan passed.

Back in India at the end of May, Mountbatten embarked on a series of meetings to win groups over to the plan. He knew that Congress approved because they would easily gain control of a single Indian state, especially without the poor Muslim areas, and if Dominion status was less than they hoped for, no one could stop them dropping it once the handover ceremonies had been forgotten. (India became a republic in 1950; Pakistan in 1956.)

Just to be sure, Mountbatten went to see Gandhi, who was not concerned enough to break his latest vow of silence, preferring to write comments on the backs of envelopes. For the Sikhs, Balder Singh, now defence minister, had no alternative and had to agree.

Jinnah, too, was in a corner. There would be a single, but two-part, state of Pakistan. However, the almost inevitable partitions of Bengal and Punjab would mean it was no more than the area he had previously described as 'moth-eaten'. Moreover, the regional Muslim leaders were more than ready to do their own independence deals to secure their local power. This was, however, the best deal he was going to get and within 24 hours Jinnah had given his agreement.

On the evening of 3 June Mountbatten and the leaders went on All-India Radio to announce that a plan for the future of India and Pakistan had been agreed. The tone was hardly celebratory. The underlying message was that it was all that could now be rescued from the situation. Jinnah did attempt to end on a positive note with the phrase *'Pakistan Zindabad'* – 'Long Live Pakistan' – but with poor radio reception, it was heard as 'Pakistan's in the bag', which sounded falsely triumphal and further antagonised Hindus.

The precise date for the transfer of power appears to have been overlooked at first. According to authors Larry Collins and Dominique Lapierre (*Freedom at Midnight*, 1975), Mountbatten claimed to have been unprepared for the question at a press conference about the 3 June plan but improvised brilliantly in order to maintain his image of confidence. He instantly chose 15 August because it was the second anniversary of the Japanese surrender which ended the Second World War. With hindsight, the anniversary of a surrender was perhaps not the date to associate with the retreat of the British from India.

More significantly, it soon emerged that according to Hindu astrologers, 15 August 1947 was so horrendously inauspicious that a compromise had to be found. The transfer would take place at the stroke of midnight, which might be regarded as the moment between the two days.

According to historian Lawrence James, '[Mountbatten's] declaration that the date of transfer or power would be brought forward to 15 August, and the Punjab was to be divided between India and Pakistan, added immeasurably to the turmoil.'

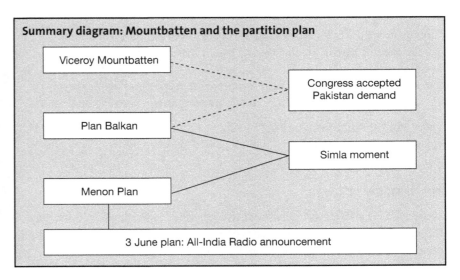

**Summary diagram: Mountbatten and the partition plan**

- Viceroy Mountbatten
- Plan Balkan
- Menon Plan
- Congress accepted Pakistan demand
- Simla moment
- 3 June plan: All-India Radio announcement

# ② Partition and independence

▶ *How were the borders between the two states decided?*

The plan only dealt with very high-level constitutional matters. Its announcement suddenly concentrated minds on what it meant for millions of human beings and for the division of administrative and military equipment. The small group deciding where the borders of the new states would fall worked in secret in case of panic and disorder.

## The Sikhs

The situation of the 6 million Sikhs was complicated and dangerous. Sikhs had dispersed across India (and the world), but were concentrated in the Punjab, where the city of Amritsar was holy to them. Relations between Sikhs and Muslims were never friendly. The prospect for the hundreds of thousands of Sikhs in the future Pakistan was not good.

The Sikh political party, the Panthic Pratinidhi, gained 22 seats in the Punjabi assembly in the 1946 elections and the party leader, Tara Singh, claimed the right to autonomy. In fact, Jinnah offered autonomy within Pakistan but this was emphatically rejected. There was, however, no realistic prospect of a third, independent Sikh state.

During 1947 communal violence escalated in the Punjab, with Sikhs particularly fearful of the paramilitary Muslim guards. Tens of thousands of Sikhs began to move out of what would be Pakistani territory. The provincial government began to disintegrate.

The 3 June plan made no particular provision for the Sikhs despite promises of special consideration. Balder Singh was scorned for giving it his support. Local leaders spoke of uprising and civil war.

Rumours about the line of the eventual border raised tensions even more. In particular, the arrival of official army troops in the mainly Sikh district of Ferozepur meant that trouble was expected, which suggested it had been included in Pakistan, which in turn meant that Amritsar itself was at best surrounded by Muslim Pakistan or fully incorporated (see the map on page 131).

In fact, while this had been true for a while, the territory around Amritsar had been clearly marked for India but the troops had not been recalled. This one small area would be a flashpoint.

## The princely states

The legal position of the princely states was perhaps more complicated than the Sikh situation, although hardly so dangerous. Strictly speaking, it was not even possible to talk of a collective position. Each of the 561 rulers had a separate treaty with the British, indeed a separate kind of treaty depending on the size and character of the princely state. With the departure of the British, each ruler was free to decide his own position. For a few states of huge size and wealth, continued independence was a tantalising possibility.

The British had no power to transfer a treaty even if the ruler wished it. Moreover, the nations of India and Pakistan did not yet exist and the princely states could not conclude new treaties with non-existent countries. So it looked unlikely that the transfer of power from the British to the Indian and Pakistani governments could also include a complete decision about the political map of the subcontinent.

In light of this, it is remarkable that, in fact, hundreds of years of princely autonomy were abandoned so quickly and so easily. Two legal principles were key: **paramountcy** and **accession**.

## Paramountcy

India had for hundreds of years been subject to a fluctuating mixture of foreign and regional powers but there was no historical precedent for power to be relinquished or gained on a single day. Congress seized the constitutional initiative. It claimed that it should now be recognised as the paramount power and opened negotiations with the princely states in the future Indian territory. There was no objection: there were no realistically autonomous states in the future Pakistani territory and, it quickly transpired, the states themselves were ready to reach new arrangements.

## Accession

In overall diplomatic terms, it was maintained that no decisions need be taken before 15 August. After that, the princely states would be able to conclude formal treaties with the constituted states of India and Pakistan. Out of diplomatic courtesy, it was maintained that such treaties might indeed recognise the independence of the princely state in question. However, states were welcome to accede to the new nations.

This courtesy actually permitted Congress, and Mountbatten, to work hard behind the scenes to push states to become part of India. Congress set up a states department to handle approaches to, and negotiations with, each of the rulers. For the time being, Congress's criticism of the lack of democracy in the princely states was suspended.

## Pressure

At the same time, all the small states without access to the sea were forced to confront their geographical weakness. Mountbatten assisted Congress by ruthlessly pressurising the rulers, publicly and privately. At a meeting of the chamber of princes on 25 July, he presented a scenario of constant fighting between local warlords with private armies, as in China. He wrote to each prince,

**KEY TERMS**

**Paramountcy** Being most important or supreme.

**Accession** The process of peacefully merging into a larger country.

telling them that his cousin, the king, would be personally insulted if they did not choose to become part of the new Dominion of India. He blithely promised that they would be free to become independent again if India became a republic, ignoring the fact that by then British promises would have no legal power.

This combination of Congress courtesy and royal arm-twisting resulted in a mass movement among the princes to accede to India. The princes would be allowed to stay as local rulers, with residual pomp and power to levy local taxes. India would be responsible for their defence and foreign relations and the territory would be officially part of India. As such, it has been calculated that Patel and Menon added more land to India than would be 'lost' by the creation of Pakistan.

## The plan in reality

Earlier in the day of 3 June, the British had presented a dossier to Indian leaders entitled 'The Administrative Consequences of Partition'. Despite its bland title, it opened the final bitter and bloody phase of the independence struggle. The dossier outlined matters for decision such as geographical boundaries, diplomatic representation, division of armed forces, civil departments, assets including railways, justice and the courts.

### Decisions about decisions

The arguments started at the very next meeting over the prior question of who was responsible for making the decisions. Congress argued that it was for Indians to decide; Jinnah that it was for the British to decide how to dispose of their colonial property. He knew that the Muslims were unlikely to obtain as much from Congress as from the British. However, Mountbatten sided with Congress, arguing that the governor-general in council – that is, he himself – was now executive officer of the Indian ministers of the interim government. Their decisions, ratified by the chief justice of India, would be final. Since Congress dominated the interim government, they would be Congress decisions and that, in effect, meant Sardar Patel decisions.

Congress forced confrontation of another issue. In their view, it was nonsense to think that India was being created. India existed and would continue. It was Pakistan which did not yet exist and therefore it was another nonsense to describe provinces joining a state which did not exist. They were seceding from India. Accordingly, if that was their choice they did not deserve any of India's assets.

### Other attitudes

Many tried to be optimistic about the partition. Mountbatten was told by an adviser that if he had not transferred power when he did, there would have been no power to transfer. Maulana Azad, the Congress Muslim leader, expressed a common view that: 'The division is only of the map of the country and not in the hearts of the people and I am sure it is going to be a short-lived partition.' There were also hard-line attitudes: some Hindus were opposed to any partition even if voted for by provincial governments, and some Muslims demanded that the historic Muslim capital of Delhi be part of Pakistan whatever the local wish (which was likely to be for India).

## Provincial decisions

As set out in the 3 June plan, assemblies of the affected provinces held votes to determine which of the future states they would join:

- Sind and Baluchistan voted with straightforward majorities for being part of a Pakistani state.
- In the complex communal provinces of Bengal and Punjab, Muslim representatives voted for undivided provinces to be in Pakistan, whereas the Hindu and (Punjabi) Sikh representatives voted for partition so that their majority areas might be in India. The provinces would accordingly be divided.
- In the North West Frontier Province, a full plebiscite was held because it was recognised that there was considerable support for Congress or even the creation of a separate tribal area: 'Pakhtunistan'. The Muslim majority decision was to be part of Pakistan.

### The Independence Act

With these decisions, the way was open to frame the independence bill, which would create the two new states. This was done in a matter of days, even including securing the agreement of both Congress and the Muslim League to the wording in advance of parliamentary discussion. On 3 July the India Committee of the British government worked until midnight to finalise the bill, which was printed during the night and presented to the House of Commons on the morning of 4 July. It was passed immediately without amendment, let alone objection, and became law in mid-July.

## Assets and the partition council

A dedicated partition council was set up in June 1947 to reach decisions on the division of the assets currently belonging to the British in India. Every item, from steam locomotives down to typewriters, had to be apportioned. More acutely, every single administrator and civil servant would have to choose to be deployed to one new country or the other.

On the partition council, Sardar Patel and Rajandra Prasad represented Congress; Liaquat Ali Khan and Abdur Rab Nishtar, quickly replaced by Jinnah, represented the Muslim League. The partition council became in effect the government of (British) India because there was no other more important business now than deciding this division. (The geographical division was out of Indian hands.) On 19 July the interim government formally split into two interim governments, one for each of the imminent states.

Behind the public façade of two new, constitutionally equal, states, Congress exerted maximum control on the basis that Pakistan was seceding and forfeited any right to Indian property. Similarly, any officials who selected employment in the future Pakistan were immediately ejected from their workplaces. The planning for Pakistan was undertaken in tent offices with scarcely any equipment.

For this reason, Liaquat Ali Khan wanted partition, if not actual independence, brought forward two weeks to 1 August. This attitude runs counter to the argument that Mountbatten is the one who should be held responsible for the rush to independence and partition. However, there is no escaping the partisanship he displayed over the decisions about post-independence governor-generals.

## Governor-general

India and Pakistan were to become separate Dominions within the Commonwealth. As such, they would retain the British monarch as head of state, with a constitutional and legislative structure like Britain of the Crown-in-Parliament. They would retain a governor-general to represent the Crown element in their own territories. The invitation to become governor-general would be made by the states immediately after the independence ceremonies but, clearly, advance plans needed to be prepared.

Mountbatten had assumed that he would become governor-general of both the successor states. He considered this would show proper care and impartiality. This was despite his evident antipathy to Jinnah, the Muslim League and Pakistan, and his lack of concern about their treatment by Congress in the partition council decisions.

Jinnah wrong-footed him with a radical but rational decision. He declared that there was no need for a British governor-general and that he would bear the responsibility himself. It was clear to the Muslims that a weak Pakistan would only come under more pressure from having the same governor-general as a strong, hostile India. Mountbatten now found himself at the receiving end of the same *realpolitik* that he had supported when it was Congress exerting the control and pressure. He was faced with the choice of resigning, impartially, on independence day or revealing his favoured relationship with India. He chose to keep the governor-generalship of India. According to historian Patrick French, 'It was a grave mistake and one that was to damage his reputation and cause great harm to Pakistan in the months ahead.' The decision revealed the long-suspected bias in favour of Congress and India.

Mountbatten was also forced to acquiesce when Jinnah pointed out that George **R.I.**, the King's official title, would no longer be acceptable in Pakistan since the 'I' clearly had no further basis in constitutional reality.

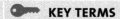 **KEY TERMS**

**Realpolitik** A term for hard-headed pragmatism, borrowed from the German language.

**R.I.** *Rex Imperator*, Latin for King-Emperor.

## The Boundary Commission

As early as February 1946, Viceroy Wavell had defined a specific line of demarcation between future Indian and Pakistani territory. No further work was done until the partition council commissioned an independent British lawyer to draw up proposals. Sir Cyril Radcliffe KC (King's Counsel) arrived in New Delhi on 8 July, 36 days before independence, and hid himself away in order to create an air of neutral consideration of maps and statistics, rather than listening to political arguments.

Two separate boundary commissions were established, one for the border between West Pakistan and India and one for the border around East Pakistan. The former involved the partition of the Punjab, the latter the partition of Bengal. Each commission had two Muslim and two non-Muslim high court judges with Radcliffe as chairperson to exercise the decisive casting vote in the event of split decisions.

### Criteria

The commissions used census data to identify the majority community in each **district** of the relevant provinces along the provisional demarcation line. They then tried to ensure that the districts of a particular majority could be grouped so as not to leave any district surrounded by a different communal majority. Every district should be **contiguous** at some point with a district of the same majority.

It was recognised, however, that the 1941 census would be out of date and might be seriously wrong in the case of the Punjab, in particular, since many Sikhs had been away in the army at the time.

### Assumptions

Various assumptions surrounded the issue of boundaries. These were never really dispelled because what emerged was never actually publicised for discussion. It was simply announced by the British as a fact.

In the first place, Jinnah had from the start of the Pakistan demand been careful not to get involved in discussions about actual borders. Nothing was done to dispel hopes of a so-called 'greater Pakistan', including undivided provinces of Punjab and Bengal and perhaps even reaching Delhi in the east. It was on the basis of this unconfirmed idea that the elections of 1946 had taken place.

There was a Congress assumption, as previously noted, that Pakistan could be 'given away' because it would fairly quickly come to its senses and be reintegrated.

The most widespread assumption was that the borders would be largely theoretical or **cartographical**. It was assumed that, in practice, people would come and go across the border freely. The precise line might appear to cut villages off from their fields, for example, but farmers would simply live in one

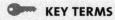

**KEY TERMS**

**District** A formal subdivision of a province.

**Contiguous** A formal term for touching or adjoining.

**Cartographical** Relating to maps.

country and work in another a few hundred metres away. Certainly, middle-class Muslims, such as Jinnah, intended to keep homes in India as well as Pakistan and travel frequently between them. On this assumption, it was felt even in June 1947 that independence might arrive without confirmed decisions which could all be worked out in due course.

In the end, Mountbatten did indeed postpone the announcement of the frontiers until after the independence ceremonies. Although he claimed to have no knowledge of the details, he had realised that there would be trouble which would quickly take the joy out of the celebrations.

### Problems

The borders determined by Radcliffe were basically the same as those secretly drawn up by Wavell in 1946. The unexpected and tragic reactions created by their notification are dealt with in the next section. A number of other unanticipated decisions were taken too. On the eastern edge of East Pakistan, a tribal area called the Chittagong Hill Tracts, which was neither Muslim nor Hindu, was awarded to Pakistan. The main reason appears to have been to

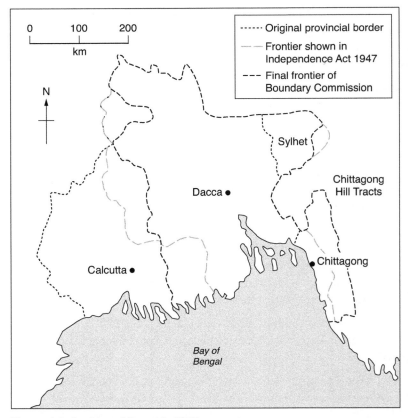

**Figure 6.1** Partition of Bengal in 1947.

include the port of Chittagong within East Pakistan, which was not going to include the great Bengal port of Calcutta. Indeed, to create an Indian zone around Calcutta, a small Muslim area to its north was awarded to India.

In the Punjab, the key problem was that Amritsar district, containing the holy city of the Sikhs, was largely surrounded by Muslim-majority districts. In addition, for a while, even Ferozepur district, despite being a Sikh-majority area, had been marked for Pakistan (see the map on page 131). It was decided to award a small portion of Lahore district to India, even though Lahore city itself was to be in Pakistan. In addition, the Gurdaspur and Ferozepur districts were placed on the Indian side of the line. However, additional troops had already been sent to Ferozepur district in anticipation of trouble. The plans were changed but this was, of course, unknown to the local population, who were alarmed by the arrival of the troops. The alarm would escalate throughout the province and lead to terrible massacres.

There is confusion and controversy to this day about this small but tragic detail of partition. Radcliffe destroyed all his notes on completion of his task so his reasoning is not known. Historian Patrick French argues that the original allocation of Ferozepur to Pakistan was in order to ensure that the headwaters of the Sutlej river were protected from diversion into Indian Punjab irrigation. Wolpert argues that Gurdaspur was reallocated to India to protect the last Indian strategic road route up to Kashmir. This princely state had not yet decided its future but the later revelation of this change has led many to see a plan to force Kashmir to accede to India (see page 130). According to historian Lawrence James, 'This murky business was finally explained in 1992 [by the secretary to the Commission]. Nehru it appears was being kept well abreast of the deliberations … and was able to induce Mountbatten to exert pressure on Radcliffe.'

One other area of dispute was the Andaman Islands, lying off Burma. During the war, these islands had been given to the Indian National Army by the invading Japanese. Now Congress claimed them for India. The Muslim League argued that if there was to be no land connection between the two halves of Pakistan, then they should be granted the islands as a refuelling base. The British also wanted them as a strategic base in the Indian Ocean since they were about to lose the entire subcontinent and all its naval dockyards.

## Independence arrives

At the stroke of midnight between 14 and 15 August 1947 the British Raj came to an end and the two nations of India and Pakistan came into existence.

Mountbatten had attended ceremonies with Jinnah in Karachi on 14 August but was firmly back in India by evening. Nehru went on All-India Radio to make one of the most poetic, apparently unscripted, political speeches in history (see Source B).

What attitudes to the past and future does Nehru express in Source B?

**SOURCE B**

**From Nehru's speech to India, night of 14/15 August, quoted in Ansar Hussain Khan, *The Rediscovery of India: A New Subcontinent*, Orient Blackswan, 1999, p. 191.**

*Long years ago we made a tryst with destiny, and now the time comes when we shall redeem our pledge, not wholly or in full measure, but very substantially.*

*At the stroke of the midnight hour, when the world sleeps, India will awake to life and freedom. A moment comes, which comes but rarely in history, when we step out from the old to the new, then an age ends, and when the soul of a nation, long suppressed, finds utterance.*

*It is fitting that at this solemn moment we take the pledge of dedication to the service of India and her people and to the still larger cause of humanity …*

*Freedom and power bring responsibility. The responsibility rests upon this assembly, a sovereign body representing the sovereign people of India. Before the birth of freedom we have endured all the pains of labour and our hearts are heavy with the memory of this sorrow. Some of those pains continue even now. Nevertheless, the past is over and it is the future that beckons to us now …*

*The ambition of the greatest man of our generation has been to wipe every tear from every eye. That may be beyond us, but as long as there are tears and suffering, so long our work will not be over.*

*A new star rises, the star of freedom in the east, a new hope comes into being, a vision long cherished materialises. May the star never set and that hope never be betrayed!*

## Radcliffe departs

Radcliffe left India on 17 August as the border decisions were announced. There was widespread condemnation. As the scale of the human consequences became apparent to the world, the newly formed United Nations launched an inquiry. Radcliffe argued that he could not be held personally responsible for the aftermath. His task had been to make recommendations to the viceroy, whose responsibility it was to reject them or accept and announce them. Radcliffe was so appalled at being made the scapegoat that he refused to accept payment for the job done.

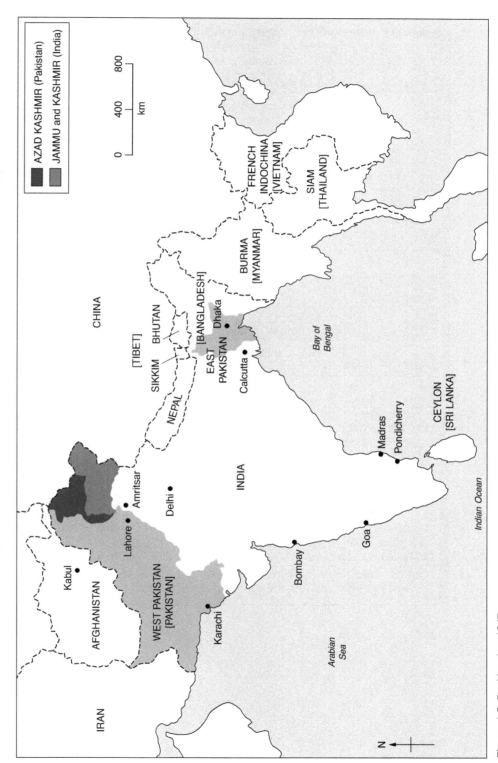

**Figure 6.2** Final borders 1947.

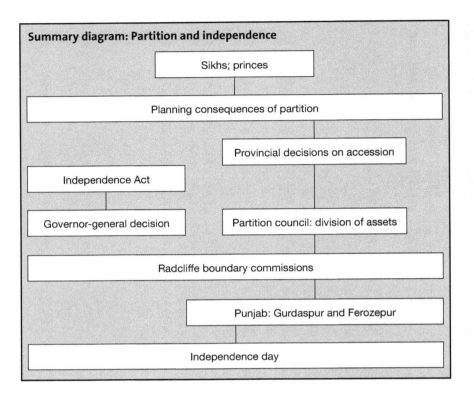

**Summary diagram: Partition and independence**

Sikhs; princes

Planning consequences of partition

Provincial decisions on accession

Independence Act

Governor-general decision

Partition council: division of assets

Radcliffe boundary commissions

Punjab: Gurdaspur and Ferozepur

Independence day

## Other imperial matters

The remaining French colonial possessions in India – mainly coastal cities including primarily Pondicherry – were not absorbed into India until 1954.

Portugal, under the Salazar dictatorship, refused to negotiate over its colonial cities, including Goa. They were eventually invaded and annexed by India in 1961 (see page 151).

Burma, which had become a separate territory of the British Empire in 1937 as a provision of the 1935 Government of India Act, became independent in 1948 and was later named Myanmar (although this is contested).

Ceylon, not actually part of British India although part of the British Empire, became independent in 1948 and was renamed Sri Lanka.

# British withdrawal and communal violence

▶ *What were the effects and consequences of partition?*

## Migrations and massacres

Mountbatten and Auchinleck (now supreme commander of all armed forces in both India and Pakistan) had agreed that the priority for remaining British troops was to protect an early withdrawal of Europeans from the subcontinent. Accordingly, Auchinleck began the process of recalling troops on 15 August. However, there was no violence directed at British troops or civilians during the departure phase. It quickly became clear that fear, anger and revenge would be intensely communal. It is debatable whether this was because the secretary of state, Listowel, had made a statement that troops would not intervene in any communal disturbances after independence. The broken Indian and Pakistan armies were not in a position to take up maintenance of order.

As a consequence, armed militias arose to protect and to intimidate. In the Punjab, Sikhs organised into *jathas* of about 30 men operating outside the law and across borders as they thought necessary. A semi-formal, multi-religious Punjab boundary force, about 20,000 strong, came together but could not protect over 17,000 villages.

On 14 August, 38 Sikhs at Lahore train station, waiting to travel out of what was about to become part of Pakistan, were knifed to death. Later the same day, a Muslim mob set fire to a *gurdwara* in Lahore, burning to death hundreds of Sikhs gathered inside for protection.

The next day, independence day, Muslim women in the Indian Punjab were dragged into the streets, stripped, raped and hacked to death. On 20 August militiamen of the Punjab boundary force shot dead 84 participants in a Muslim mob. On 24 August Muslim members of the force were killed by their fellow Hindu soldiers, after having shot Hindu looters. The force split along communal lines and on 1 September was broken up completely. There was no law and order in the Punjab for weeks on end.

### Massacres

Massacres of whole villages began. Thousands were killed every day. As fear and panic spread, millions of people left their homes to attempt to reach the relative safety of the other country of their co-religionists. As they walked in endless lines, they were even more vulnerable to attack.

Most infamous were the trains pulling into their destinations without a living passenger, the thousands of refugees aboard having been massacred and sent

**KEY TERMS**

**Jatha** A squad.
**Gurdwara** Sikh temple.

on their way. A reporter for *The Times* watched a train full of 4000 Muslims being carefully shunted into a station siding in preparation for a cold-blooded massacre.

Criminal gangs preyed on migrants; death squads worked through lists of names to clear neighbourhoods. Victims were publicly humiliated, tortured and genitally mutilated before being killed. As law and order disintegrated and thousands of bodies were left to rot in the August heat, cholera and other diseases spread rapidly, causing more fear and flight. It is said that the vultures were too fat to fly.

**SOURCE C**

? Why do you think the refugees in Source C were prepared to risk their lives trying to escape by train?

**Refugee trains in the Punjab in 1947.**

## Mass rape

Mass rape was used as a weapon of war. Hindu, Sikh and Muslim women alike committed suicide when surrounded, often by throwing themselves down well shafts. In some cases, men killed their families rather than let the mobs get to them. Women and girls were also abducted, forcibly converted and 'married'. Even when located in later years, the women were afraid to return to their own communities because of what they had been forced into.

The personal and financial strain of the refugee crisis was intolerable. More than half a million refugees arrived in Indian Punjab, making the province bankrupt. Hundreds of thousands struggled on to Delhi, barely surviving in squalid camps where women and girls were sold in exchange for food.

## Death toll

All the authorities publicly underestimated the death toll. The British preferred it to be seen as continuing unrest but on a larger scale; they did not want to be accused of causing, and then turning their back on, an unprecedented human catastrophe. The Indian and Pakistani governments quite simply wanted to avoid inflaming the situation or appearing incompetent. At the time, it was said that 200,000 died; a figure of about a million is now regarded as more accurate.

**SOURCE D**

**A cartoon by Leslie Illingworth published in the *Daily Mail*, 20 May 1947, about the violence surrounding partition.**

What do the various central figures in Source D represent?

The massacres left a psychological scar across the political act of partition and the birth of the two independent nations. In the Punjab, it was nothing less than civil war, and in the opinion of some, communal genocide. The dubious current term of 'ethnic cleansing' would certainly be applied: less than one per cent of the population of Pakistani Punjab is Hindu or Sikh and less than one per cent of the Indian Punjab population is Muslim.

## The princely states

On independence, India and Pakistan were able to conclude legal treaties with the princely states. Within two years, as a result of the determined negotiations of Menon and Patel, all but three of the 561 states had acceded to what was termed the Indian Union. Only three states resisted: Junagadh, Hyderabad and Kashmir.

## Junagadh

The Nawab of Junagadh, a small coastal state in the north-west, had opted to accede to Pakistan on independence even though the two were separated by 500 km of Indian territory. Mountbatten had not argued against this plan when he was still viceroy. Patel had other ideas. He ordered the Indian Army to blockade the state, threatening mass starvation. The Nawab fled by sea to Pakistan, the army 'invaded' and a quick plebiscite resulted in an overwhelming popular vote to join the Indian Union.

## Hyderabad

The Nizam of Hyderabad declined to join either India or Pakistan on the principle that modern nation-states should not be formed for religious reasons. Although landlocked in the centre of the subcontinent, he could afford this high-minded stance because Hyderabad covered tens of thousands of square metres (larger than many members of the United Nations) and had its own army, and the Nizam was then the richest man in the world. He was able to lend the new Pakistan government 200 million rupees without hesitation. It was agreed that there should be a one-year 'standstill agreement'. After the departure of Mountbatten (in 1948), Nehru and Patel ordered the annexation of the state, the army invaded (really invaded, unlike Junagadh, since the ruler resisted) and after four days of fighting the Nizam gave in.

## Kashmir

The problem of Kashmir has still not been resolved. Kashmir was a large, mixed princely state right up against the mountains of the Hindu Kush and the Himalaya where the Indus river of Pakistan begins. The population was 80 per cent Muslim but was ruled by a Hindu Maharajah, Hari Singh, from his court at Srinagar. However, the Muslims were of a different (Sufi) tradition to the Muslims of the Punjab, now Pakistan. In addition, there was a considerable Buddhist population in the Ladakh area.

Kashmir adjoined the Punjab and if that had become wholly Pakistani there would have been no border with India. The partition of the Punjab resulted in some contiguity with the post-independence province of Himachal Pradesh but only through mountainous territory. Most land routes into upper Kashmir were through Pakistani territory, except one, through the controversial Gurdaspur district.

It made sense, both demographically and geographically, for Kashmir to join Pakistan. The Maharajah for his part seems to have thought that the British would never actually leave. When it came to pass, he attempted to model the state's future on Switzerland's neutrality. When that failed, he opted for India: some say because he feared that Kashmir would suffer communal violence as had Punjab and Bengal; some say his family feared to live in an Islamic state.

## Provocations

The events in Kashmir of 1947–8 are controversial to this day and subject to differing nationalist interpretations. According to the Indian version, Hari Singh tried to secure a standstill agreement as in Hyderabad, to which Pakistan agreed but India did not. Pakistan then applied economic pressure for a decision by restricting supplies along the roads in Pakistani territory. On the night of 21/22 October 1947 Pathan irregular troops, led by Pakistani officers, entered Kashmir and proceeded towards Srinagar. The border areas of which they took

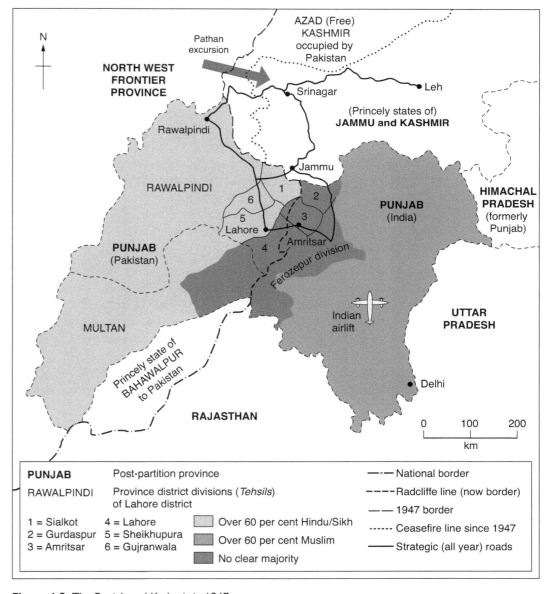

**Figure 6.3** The Punjab and Kashmir in 1947.

control are still occupied by Pakistani troops and are marked on maps as Azad (Free) Kashmir.

According to the Pakistani version, Kashmiri troops had been harassing Muslims out of Kashmiri villages along the border with Pakistan in order to create a depopulated zone which was easier to protect. It was this harassment which provoked the Pathans to come to their support.

## Divergent motives

From this point, there also appear to be divergences in British and Indian motives. Hari Singh appealed for Indian military assistance, which Patel was prepared to organise. Nehru, whose family originally came from Kashmir, is often thought to have secretly arranged for Kashmir to become Indian. In fact, he repeatedly blocked Singh's request on a matter of democratic principle.

One popular Muslim leader in Kashmir, Sheikh Abdullah, had been imprisoned by the Maharajah. Nehru demanded that Singh release Abdullah and hold a plebiscite to determine transparently the wishes of the people. Nehru was prepared to accept that the overall vote might be for Pakistan. He also argued that if it was for India then whatever land the Pathans had occupied could be retaken. Singh refused to release Abdullah. Mountbatten, now governor-general of India, sided with Patel's wish to intervene on the narrow legal grounds that princes were free to decide the fate of their states without plebiscites. However, he would not agree to military assistance until Hari Singh had signed the accession document.

It now appears to some historians that the British government, as distinct from Mountbatten, really wanted Kashmir to belong to Pakistan. Kashmir was the most northerly area of the former Raj. Britain retained a strategic interest, supported by the USA, in monitoring Soviet and Chinese activity across the border. Britain trusted Muslim Pakistan more than an India governed by Nehru, whose policy of non-alignment (see page 151) meant he was just as friendly to the Soviet Union and Communist China as to Britain and the USA. Attlee repeatedly refused to support Mountbatten's hasty actions in support of India.

Memoirs of Pakistani generals have revealed that a further strategic interest was the major road running along the Pakistani side of the border between Lahore and the army headquarters at Rawalpindi. An Indian Kashmir could allow India to invade and cut off troop reinforcements to the Punjab in a matter of hours.

Two matters remain confused:

- the accession document
- the Gurdaspur district.

## The accession document

The records show a flurry of plane flights between Delhi and Srinagar culminating apparently in a signed accession document, accompanied by a promise from Hari Singh to Nehru that he would release Abdullah and hold a plebiscite. The United Nations has repeatedly called for this plebiscite to be held but India refuses to organise it until Pakistani troops withdraw from Azad Kashmir.

Indian troops were airlifted into Srinagar, saved the Maharaja and held the Pathans back. Whether the airlift started before the accession was actually signed remains a question. There seems reason to believe that Patel pulled the wool over Nehru's eyes for a crucial few hours and days. The accession was certainly claimed as the reason why the (British) commander-in-chief of the Pakistan Army refused to commit Pakistani troops when the Indian Army entered Kashmir.

### The Gurdaspur district

It was recalled that the Punjabi Muslim-majority district of Gurdaspur was actually put on the Indian side of the border. The official reason was to ensure that Amritsar was not surrounded by Pakistani territory.

The Kashmir crisis led to an alternative theory that Mountbatten had put secret pressure on Radcliffe to ensure that the one last road and rail-link into Kashmir which stayed open throughout the winter – through Gurdaspur district – stayed in Indian territory. According to this theory, there must have been a Mountbatten–Congress plan to gain Kashmir from the start.

## The end of Gandhi and Jinnah

Gandhi had been sidelined as the political momentum gathered towards independence. He was, however, still a respected figure. As communal violence erupted, and despite his age, he took himself to the centre of disturbances. In Bengal, he walked from village to village, insisting on calm before he moved on. He did not attempt the same in the Punjab; perhaps even he thought it beyond hope for a while.

Gandhi remained constant to his lifelong view that he should and could take personal responsibility for the violence and for promoting religious tolerance by example. He continued to include readings from the **Qur'an** at his prayer meetings and deliberately chose to be in a Muslim property on independence night. He let it be known that he was so distressed by the treatment of the Muslims that he was planning to spend what remained of his life in (East) Pakistan.

This was too much for some. At 5p.m. on the evening of 30 January 1948 he was walking to his evening prayer meeting among a crowd of supporters. Three shots were fired at close range into his chest. He died within minutes. It was later claimed that his last words were a prayer to the Hindu god Ram. More credible witnesses reported self-deprecation to the end: he said he hated being late for prayers.

 **KEY TERM**

**Qur'an** The Muslim holy book.

Gandhi's assassination was long-feared and leaders braced themselves for renewed communal attacks. However, it soon became clear that his killer, Nathuram Godse, was a Hindu fanatic, incensed by Gandhi's care for Muslims. Godse was a member of the Rashtriya Swayamsewak Sangh (RSS), a murky Hindu fundamentalist organisation. Patel had tolerated the fact that many RSS supporters were in positions of party or civil authority. Now, Nehru, the lifelong anti-fascist, demanded that Patel outlaw the RSS. On Gandhi's death, Nehru broadcast on All-India Radio that 'the light has gone out of our lives and there is darkness everywhere'.

Jinnah did not outlive the same year. His lung disease worsened throughout 1948 and in September he died, aged 71, in Karachi. He had achieved a remarkable objective, despite Gandhi's opposition, and yet curiously in the end he too adopted a tolerant, all-embracing position. In August 1947 he declared, in effect, that Pakistan was a secular, not a Muslim state. He promised: 'You may belong to any religion or caste or creed – that has nothing to do with the business of the state.'

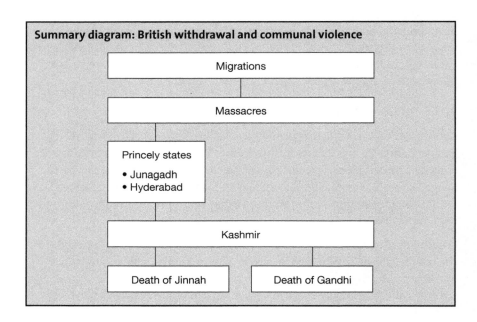

**Summary diagram: British withdrawal and communal violence**

# Key debate

▶ *A shameful flight? Did the British rush the final transfer of power?*

The Labour government in March 1947 set Mountbatten a deadline of June 1948 for the transfer of power. On 3 June 1947 Mountbatten announced a deadline of 15 August 1947. This debate concerns the question as to whether that shortening constitutes an achievement which arguably saved lives or whether it reveals an unnecessary haste which arguably led to panic and the partition massacres.

The emotive expression 'shameful flight' was first deployed by Churchill himself in the (almost emergency) parliamentary debate on the Indian Independence Bill in 1947. He said that he grieved for the 'clattering down of the British Empire' and pleaded, rhetorically, 'let us not add by shameful flight, by a premature, hurried scuttle – at least let us not add to the pangs of sorrow so many us feel, the taint and sneer of shame'.

Viceroy Mountbatten responded to the general accusation of haste in an addition to his final report on his viceroyalty. He carefully laid out what might be called the official justification in an appendix to his 'Report on the Last Viceroyalty' submitted to the British government in September 1948. He denied that the decision was hurried and emphasised the hopes that an early transfer would generate greater goodwill towards Britain in independent India, would strengthen the separating government administrations and would actually lessen the urgency of making a new constitution before independence.

This analysis is supported by other contemporary participants such as Penderel Moon (later Sir), an officer in the Indian Civil Service until 1943 and revenue minister for the state of Bahawalpur until independence (see Extract 1).

**EXTRACT I**

**From Penderel Moon, *Divide and Quit: An Eyewitness Account of the Partition of India*, Chatto & Windus, 1961, p. 282.**

*Postponement of Partition by ten months could have done no good; and it carried with it dangers of its own. Sparks from suppressed fires in the Punjab were liable to ignite combustible materials in other parts of India. Any delay in separating the armed forces might give occasion, in the excited state of feeling for clashes between Muslim and non-Muslim units with incalculable consequences. The three parties who had agreed to the Mountbatten [Menon] Plan might resile [move away from] from it, if they were given too much time for reflection. Furthermore from the purely British point of view there was the danger that the drastic measures which would be necessary for keeping the peace in the Punjab would earn them the odium [hatred] of all three communities and that they would in the end leave the country amid general execration. All things considered it must really be accounted a mercy that Lord Mountbatten did not foresee more clearly the magnitude of the calamity that threatened the Punjab.*

The final sentence is, of course, double-edged in its judgement. More directly critical is a leading international historian of Indian independence, Stanley Wolpert. He takes Churchill's accusation as the title of one of his many books on the subject: *Shameful Flight*. Wolpert is sympathetic to Jinnah and hostile to Mountbatten, or rather to 'the many laudatory, fawning accounts of Lord Mountbatten's "splendid," "historically unique," "brilliant and wonderful" viceroyalty that have … filled shelves of Partition literature and Mountbatten hagiography'. He is writing with later scholarship but includes in his opening argument a devastating self-judgement by Mountbatten himself as revealed to a BBC international correspondent.

### EXTRACT 2

**From Stanley Wolpert, *Shameful Flight, The Last Years of the British Empire in India*, Oxford University Press, 2006, pp. 1–2.**

*In … 1947 the world's mightiest modern empire … abandoned its vow to protect one-fifth of humankind. Britain's shameful flight from its Indian Empire came only ten weeks after its last viceroy … took it upon himself to cut ten months from the brief time allotted by the Labor [sic] Government's cabinet to withdraw … .*

*Prime Minister Clement Attlee and his cabinet gave Mountbatten until June of 1948 to try to facilitate agreement between the major competing political party leaders of India to work together within a single federation. But adrenaline-charged Mountbatten scuttled that last best hope of the British Imperial Raj … to leave India to single independent government, deciding instead to divide British India into fragmented dominions of India and Pakistan.*

*I believe that the tragedy of Partition might well have been avoided … or at least mitigated, but for the arrogance and ignorance of a handful of British and Indian leaders. Those ten additional months of postwar talks, aborted by an impatient Mountbatten, might have helped all parties to agree that cooperation was much wiser than conflict … .*

*When asked how he felt about his Indian viceroyalty eighteen years after Partition, Mountbatten himself admitted to BBC's John Osman … that he had … 'fucked it up.'*

Lawrence James is also critical of Mountbatten's approach but concludes his study with an attempt at compassion and understanding of the viceroy's limitations.

## EXTRACT 3

**From Lawrence James, *Raj: The Making and Unmaking of British India*, Little, Brown & Co., 1997, pp. 609.**

*In the light of his extraordinary efforts to preserve and wherever possible add lustre to his reputation, Mountbatten deserves compassion rather than condemnation. Those who tamper with history are usually frightened by it and for all his colossal vanity the Viceroy may have been conscious that on occasions his judgment had been mistaken … Mountbatten's critics [are] probably right to question his decision to end the Raj in seventy-three days and to stick unswervingly to a time-table which events revealed to be dangerously unrealistic. His treatment of the princes was shabby … As for the slaughter in the Punjab greater efforts should have been made to work out an adequate exigency plan in anticipation of a disaster which was plainly waiting to happen. And yet to condemn Mountbatten for these oversights and underhand manoeuvres is to judge him by the vision and high moral standards of, say, Curzon or Irwin. They were architects and he was a demolition engineer … Political power had all but passed into Indian hands by March 1947. Quite simply the last Viceroy lacked the prestige, authority and resources of his predecessors and, therefore, placed himself in the hands of those who possessed all these assets – Nehru and the Congress high command. He found them congenial partners and performed his duties according to his lights: the trouble was that he had too much to say for himself and no humility.*

> Study Extracts 1–3. Do you think it is fair to judge Mountbatten on what he could, or could not, have foreseen?

## Chapter summary

The Labour government was committed to transferring power in India, preferably in a unified state, with Dominion status within the Commonwealth. The new but final viceroy, Lord Louis Mountbatten, was charming, capable and a great-grandson of Queen Victoria. Mountbatten set about carrying out the instructions he had been given. His first plan had to be shelved at the last minute because of Nehru's vehement opposition to its proposal for freedom of choice by provinces and states about whether to be autonomous or join others in a series of groups across the country. This proposal for fragmentation was dubbed Plan Balkan. Another plan was hastily drawn up by a Congress politician and announced by Mountbatten, who chose a date for its implementation on the spur of the moment. The new shorter timetable meant a rush to make all the necessary decisions, although the actual division of the country was prepared in secret and only announced after the independence celebrations. Terrible massacres followed as people discovered they were not in their preferred country and tried to travel across the new border. Although most of the princely states acceded calmly, three states resisted, one of which, Kashmir, remains a flashpoint of conflict between India and Pakistan to this day.

Refresher questions

Use these questions to remind yourself of the key material covered in this chapter.

1 Why was Mountbatten appointed viceroy?
2 What were Mountbatten's priorities?
3 What deadline was Mountbatten given?
4 When did Mountbatten deliver independence?
5 What was the key feature of Plan Balkan?
6 What caused the Menon Plan to be created?
7 How would partition affect the Punjabi Sikhs?
8 How did Mountbatten and Patel deal with the Indian princes?

9 What did 'the administrative consequences of partition' consist of?
10 How were national assets to be divided?
11 What were the decisions regarding the two governors-general?
12 What were the problematic border issues?
13 What were the immediate human consequences of partition?
14 What were the outstanding provincial accession problems?

 Question practice

## ESSAY QUESTIONS

1 'Britain's "shameful flight" from India, ten months earlier than planned, aggravated the tragedy of partition.' How far do you agree with this statement?
2 How significant was the decision to postpone announcement of the border until after the moment of independence for the departing British and affected local populations?
3 'The Menon Plan averted an immediate crisis but served India badly.' How far do you agree with this statement?
4 To what extent was the accession of Kashmir free and fair to the population of the province?

## SOURCE ANALYSIS QUESTIONS

1 Why is Source 1 valuable to the historian for an enquiry into evaluating the British strategy over the demand for Pakistan? Explain your answer using the source, the information given about it and your own knowledge of the historical context.
2 How much weight do you give the evidence of Source 2 for an enquiry into the justification for bringing forward the British transfer of power to India in 1947? Explain your answer using the source, the information given about it and your own knowledge of the historical context.
3 How far could the historian make use of Sources 2 and 3 together to investigate the accusation that Britain, and Viceroy Mountbatten in particular, mismanaged the final transfer of power in the Indian subcontinent? Explain your answer using the sources, the information given about them and your own knowledge of the historical context.

---

**SOURCE 1**

**From Penderel Moon, *Divide and Quit: An Eyewitness Account of the Partition of India*, Chatto & Windus, 1961, p. 282.**

*Postponement of Partition by ten months could have done no good; and it carried with it dangers of its own. Sparks from suppressed fires in the Punjab were liable to ignite combustible materials in other parts of India. Any delay in separating the armed forces might give occasion, in the excited state of feeling for clashes between Muslim and non-Muslim units with incalculable consequences. The three parties who had agreed to the Mountbatten [Menon] Plan might resile [move away from] from it, if they were given too much time for reflection. Furthermore from the purely British point of view there was the danger that the drastic measures which would be necessary for keeping the peace in the Punjab would earn them the odium [hatred] of all three communities and that they would in the end leave the country amid general execration. All things considered it must really be accounted a mercy that Lord Mountbatten did not foresee more clearly the magnitude of the calamity that threatened the Punjab.*

---

**SOURCE 2**

**From a memorandum, dated 1945, by (Sir) Penderel Moon, an officer in the Indian Civil Service until 1943 and revenue minister for the state of Bahawalpur until independence, republished in *The Pakistan Nettle* and quoted in D.N. Panigrahi, *India's Partition*, Routledge, 2004, p. 316.**

*To come down on the side of Pakistan is likely to be the right decision. That should be our working hypothesis. We should at once begin to test reactions to this in those quarters whence the most formidable opposition may be expected. We should be ready in the last resort to throw the whole weight of our power and influence on to the side of Pakistan, if the testings confirm that this is the right decision. If the Pakistan principle is conceded, Jinnah is likely to be more reasonable and welcome arrangements for close collaboration between Hindustan and Pakistan. There is more likelihood of obtaining consent to division than Muslim consent to union. Crude considerations of British interests also point to the same conclusion. For Hindu India is already deeply estranged. Refusal of Pakistan will estrange the Muslims also.*

---

**SOURCE 3**

**From Stanley Wolpert, *Shameful Flight, The Last Years of the British Empire in India*, Oxford University Press, 2006, pp. 1–2.**

*In ... 1947 the world's mightiest modern empire ... abandoned its vow to protect one-fifth of humankind. Britain's shameful flight from its Indian Empire came only ten weeks after its last viceroy ... took it upon himself to cut ten months from the brief time allotted by the Labor [sic] Government's cabinet to withdraw ... .*

*Prime Minister Clement Attlee and his cabinet gave Mountbatten until June of 1948 to try to facilitate agreement between the major competing political party leaders of India to work together within a single federation. But adrenaline-charged Mountbatten scuttled that last best hope of the British Imperial Raj ... to leave India to single independent government, deciding instead to divide British India into fragmented dominions of India and Pakistan.*

*I believe that the tragedy of Partition might well have been avoided ... or at least mitigated, but for the arrogance and ignorance of a handful of British and Indian leaders. Those ten additional months of postwar talks, aborted by an impatient Mountbatten, might have helped all parties to agree that cooperation was much wiser than conflict ... .*

*When asked how he felt about his Indian viceroyalty eighteen years after Partition, Mountbatten himself admitted to BBC's John Osman ... that he had ... 'fucked it up.'*

## CHAPTER 7

# The Nehru years 1948–64

Independence brought the promise of democracy but that did not mean political harmony. If anything, the freedom from loyalty to the unifying cause of nationalism allowed more dissent to emerge. The power struggle now took place within Congress between right-wing figures and Nehru as champion of socialist ideas. As prime minister of the new Dominion of India, Nehru started to industrialise the country and increase food production. In foreign affairs he virtually created the non-aligned movement between the West and the Communist bloc.

This chapter examines:

★ Domestic affairs

★ International relations

## Key dates

| | | | | | |
|---|---|---|---|---|---|
| 1948 | | Departure of Mountbatten, governor-general of India | 1954 | | Chinese border provocations began |
| 1950 | Jan. 26 | India proclaimed a republic, remaining part of Commonwealth | 1955 | | Bandung Conference of the non-aligned movement |
| | | Nehru–Liaquat Pact | 1956 | | Second Five-Year Plan |
| 1951 | | First ever general election in India | 1957 | | Discovery of Chinese road through Aksai Chin |
| 1952 | | First Five-Year Plan | 1961 | | Indian military annexation of Goa |
| 1953 | | States Reorganisation Commission | 1962 | | Chinese invasion |
| | | | 1964 | | Death of Nehru |

## 1 Domestic affairs

▶ *How successful were Nehru's domestic policies?*

### Power struggle

In 1948 Nehru found himself dealing with former political allies manoeuvring against him. Nehru had always been a socialist but loyal to Congress. He was now denounced by socialists within Congress saying that Congress 'had outlived its utility'. The socialists warned that Congress was 'in danger, because it has an authoritarian bias, of being overwhelmed by anti-secular, anti-democratic forces of the Right'. Rather than stay to fight for the control of Congress, they chose to split from Congress to form a separate Socialist Party. Nehru had lost valuable allies in the struggle to maintain Congress as a broad inclusive organisation.

During the period 1948–51 Nehru's power and influence declined. Powerful Congress figures such as Sardar Patel, deputy prime minister, Rajendra Prasad, first president of India, and Syama Mookerjee, another minister, were sympathetic to the view that Congress was really a Hindu organisation. This was an issue which had been kept in the background during the years of struggle against the British. Both Gandhi and Nehru had been proud of the Muslim membership of Congress (however small). Gandhi's attitude frequently became patronising about Muslims whereas Nehru was vehemently opposed to communal politics in principle and saw Congress as above religious loyalties. He abhorred the idea that Congress should use its power in support of the Hindu religion.

Patel had proposed that members of the right-wing extremist Hindu organisation RSS be invited to join Congress, claiming that this would moderate them. The assassination of Gandhi by RSS members meant he actually had to ban them but he soon got the ban lifted the following year, in 1949. Prasad did not want the army to protect victimised Muslims because it would make the government unpopular. Nehru argued that India's new freedom had little meaning if standards of justice were based on popularity. Nevertheless, he could not secure a balanced approach over pro-Hindu measures. For example, the protection of cows, sacred animals to Hindus, from slaughter had long been an objective of Congress Hindus, but had been blocked by Gandhi as too narrowly Hindu. With Gandhi dead, this was now enacted.

The power struggle between Nehru and Patel dominated Congress politics. Against Nehru's objections, Patel made it a part of the constitution that the princes who had lost their states on independence should be financially compensated for life. He also blocked Nehru's socialist attempts to abolish the *zamindar* class.

 **KEY TERM**

*Zamindar* A landowner taking rent from peasant farmers.

On 26 January 1950 India converted to a republic, although remaining within the Commonwealth. As a republic, the country would have a president. Nehru wanted Rajagopalachari to be the interim president, but Patel manoeuvred Prasad into position. Nehru did at least manage to stop Prasad determining his inauguration date through Hindu astrologers.

In addition, the post of Congress president was contested. Nehru ruled himself out since he was prime minister but was unenthusiastic about either of the two main candidates, Kripalani and Tandon. Tandon was an extreme pro-Hindu politician who wanted the Hindi language purified of foreign elements, including Western numerals. He had stated that Muslims, if not converting,

# Jawaharlal Nehru

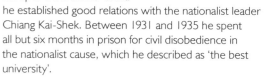

| | |
|---|---|
| 1889 | Born in Allahabad, northern India |
| 1904 | Educated at Harrow public school in England |
| 1907 | Studied at Cambridge University, then trained as a barrister |
| 1921 | First imprisonment |
| 1929 | President of Congress |
| 1946 | Head of interim government; vice-president of governor-general's Executive Council |
| 1947–64 | Prime minister of India; known as Pandit ('Teacher') Nehru |
| 1964 | Died |

Jawaharlal 'beautiful jewel' Nehru was born into a prosperous Kashmiri Brahmin family. His father, Motilal, was an intellectual and a politician. He was an only child until he was eleven years old. In 1916 he was married to Kamala (died 1936) and his daughter Indira was born in 1918.

It was the Amritsar Massacre that aroused Nehru's interest in politics. During the non-cooperation movements his concern for the poor grew with his popular appeal. Nehru believed passionately in modern secular democracy, with equal rights for women, and was a lifelong socialist. He has been called 'a Brahmin who loathed caste'. He wanted independence for India more for the chance to improve the lives of the population than just personal political pride.

In the 1920s Nehru visited Europe and Soviet Russia, which impressed him particularly. In the 1930s he was horrified by fascist Europe. On a visit to China he established good relations with the nationalist leader Chiang Kai-Shek. Between 1931 and 1935 he spent all but six months in prison for civil disobedience in the nationalist cause, which he described as 'the best university'.

Nehru was the protégé of Gandhi, who described him as 'pure as crystal, he is truthful beyond suspicion. He is a knight [without fear, without dishonour]. The nation is safe in his hands.' However, the increasing emphasis Gandhi placed on religion and Hinduism strained their relationship. Nevertheless, Gandhi, the visionary, and Nehru, the politician, have been compared to Marx, the thinker, and Lenin, the achiever.

Nehru was a lonely man but much loved – publicly by the Indian masses and privately by the famous – Sarojini Padmaja Naidu, Lady Edwina Mountbatten, Madame Chiang Kai-Shek and Jacqueline Kennedy.

Nehru's daughter Indira later married a Gandhi (no relation) and created a new Indian dynasty by becoming prime minister. She was assassinated by her Sikh bodyguard in revenge for her ordering an armed assault on Sikh separatists occupying Amritsar's Golden Temple in 1984.

must at least adopt Hindu cultural appearances and practices. Tandon succeeded and this galvanised Nehru into a fightback.

## Fightback

Nehru warned Tandon that he would not tolerate any pro-Hindu interference in economic policy. Moreover, Nehru introduced the Hindu Code Bill into Parliament, seeking to modernise elements of Hindu social law. Tandon opposed the Bill from within Congress while Kripalani broke away completely to form another party. Dr Ambedkar of the Dalits resigned from the government, accusing Nehru of not standing up to Tandon. Nehru went for high stakes and resigned from the Congress Central Working Committee, the heart of the party, declaring the party must choose between him and Tandon. Congress swung behind him, Tandon resigned and Nehru became Congress president as well as prime minister.

Now Prasad, the national president, overreacted to the defeat of Tandon and announced his objections to the Hindu Code Bill. Political intervention of this kind by the president was not permitted. Nehru again threatened to resign unless Prasad accepted his limits, which he did.

In 1951 Patel, who had suffered a heart attack in 1948 when he was accused of failing to stop known plots to kill Gandhi, died, leaving Nehru without an obvious rival. Nehru had survived the departure of his allies and fought off his internal opponents. He now faced the electorate. The first general election ever held in India began on 25 October 1951. It took six months to complete, with 176 million voters in mostly rural areas, 17,000 candidates from 75 political parties fighting for 489 seats in Parliament and 3283 seats in regional assemblies.

**KEY TERM**

**Sadhu** Hindu holy man.

Congress won a landslide, soundly defeating the breakaway socialists and communalist (religious) parties. Nehru himself had been challenged in his own constituency by a **sadhu** but won a massive majority. He would remain prime minister securely until his death thirteen years later. However, India itself was not yet secure from further break-up.

## Breakaway tensions

The creation of the two wings of Pakistan was a traumatic act deserving the description of partition. However, there were several smaller areas which continued to demand autonomy or secession from independent India.

The Indian subcontinent contains about 200 languages. Ever since the 1905 partition of Bengal (see page 10), Congress had argued for the reorganisation of provinces along linguistic lines. In other words, communities speaking the same language (whatever their religious mixture) were likely to be more cohesive and less agitated. In 1937–8, Congress had formally declared the need for new language-based provinces. However, after independence and the perception of defeat over partition, Nehru and Patel led Congress into rejecting further fragmentation and the Constituent Assembly of 1946 created provinces based on administrative priorities.

In October 1952 Potti Sriramalu, a veteran of Gandhi's 1930 Salt March, started a fast unto death in order to pressurise the government into language-based reorganisation. The Congress government stood firm; in December Sriramalu died and violence flared across India. Nehru gave in and three days later the government agreed on the creation of a first language-based province. In 1953 a full States Reorganisation Commission was set up. This led to the 1956 States Reorganisation Act, creating a number of state (that is, former provincial) boundary changes to reflect language communities but without further autonomy. These included Andhra and Madhya Pradesh, Kerala, Mysore (now named Karnataka) and Madras (now named Tamil Nadu).

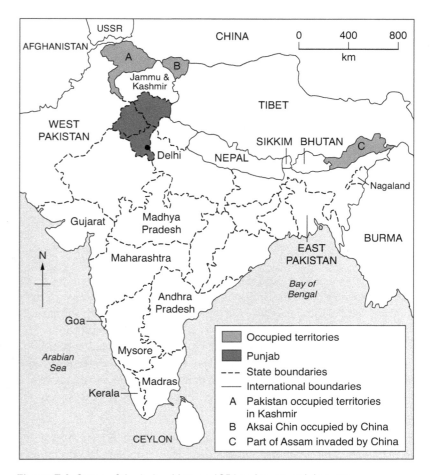

**Figure 7.1** States of the Indian Union c.1956 and territorial disputes.

## West and south

Following further rioting in 1960, the large Bombay province was split into the Marathi-speaking state of Maharashtra (capital now Mumbai) and the Gujerati-speaking Gujarat.

The Indian south is home to a whole family of languages called Dravidian. The Dravidian speakers had long regarded northern Indians as invaders or oppressors, whether Hindu or Muslim (Mughal). They regarded the decision to make Hindi the official language of independent India as **neo-imperialist**. There was (and to a certain extent still is) a secessionist movement in the far south. However, Nehru created a compromise solution by also making English an official national language (as it still is today).

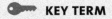 **KEY TERM**

**Neo-imperialist** A strategy of reimposing an imperial-style control, perhaps through economic power rather than military force.

## North

In the large Punjab region, Hindus spoke Hindi written in the Devanagari lettering and the more numerous Sikhs spoke Punjabi written in Gurmukhi script. The organisation Akali Dal agitated for a separate **theocratic** Sikh state. Nehru was ready to countenance a full civil war to prevent the secession of an anti-Hindu area bordering Pakistan, which would threaten access to Kashmir. The Akali Dal wanted a smaller 'purer' Sikh Punjab state. The States Commission did the opposite, merging Punjab, Himachal Pradesh and PEPSU (a state formed out of former princely states). Tara Singh, leader of the secessionist movement, began a fast unto death in August 1961 but surrendered ignominiously in October. Punjab remained loyal to India in subsequent conflicts with Pakistan although Sikh separatism would occasionally become violent in the following years (see profile on page 143).

## East

A secessionist movement which did turn into guerrilla warfare arose in the most north-eastern province of Assam, beyond East Pakistan. Zapu Phizo, leader of the Naga tribes, had collaborated with the Japanese and the Indian Nationalist Army when these forces reached the borders of India in 1944, in return for promises of independence should British India be defeated. In fact, the British Indian forces successfully resisted at the battle of Kohima (in Naga territory) and Phizo hurriedly switched sides in return for a promise of a ten-year standstill on absorption or independence. The Indian government used those years wisely, bringing roads and investment to the area.

In 1956, just before the decade was up, the Nagas created a rebel government and started guerrilla warfare in the jungle region, with arms supplied from East Pakistan. However, they were now prepared to accept a fully autonomous state within the Indian constitution. While Phizo went to Britain to get support from the media and perhaps secret service assistance also, the Indian government held local elections in 1964. When Phizo offered a ceasefire, the national government told him he must now negotiate with his fellow (moderate) Naga provincial government, which in turn refused. Phizo died in British exile and the entire movement fizzled out.

## Kashmir

The problem of Nehru's beloved Kashmir remained, and still remains, unresolved. Nehru promised to refer the dispute regarding accession (to either India or Pakistan) to the United Nations, but only on condition that Pakistani troops withdraw from territory captured in the small war of 1948. This has never happened nor is likely even 50 years after Nehru's death. The province remains unofficially partitioned. There have been numerous military clashes along the so-called line-of-control and bloody insurgency within Kashmir since 1988. Now that both India and Pakistan have nuclear weapons the dangers have increased dramatically. However, it was conflict in another part of Kashmir that damaged Nehru most (see page 153).

## Socialism

As we have seen in earlier chapters, Nehru respected Gandhi's non-violent methods but rejected his vision. Gandhi wanted the unrealistic peace of a medieval village economy and caste society; Nehru wanted progress, equality and the future. He believed in the benefits of socialism, science, technology and industry, and all of this through central planning. He was unafraid to disagree sharply with Gandhi, once writing to him: 'A village, normally speaking, is backward intellectually and culturally … Narrow-minded people are much more likely to be untruthful and violent.'

Nehru had visited the Soviet Union in the 1920s and admired its innovative Five-Year Plan for the national economy. Back in India, he argued for Congress to approve the need for change to the economic system when it gained power. Source A recounts Nehru's inaugural presidential address to Congress in 1929.

**SOURCE A**

**Nehru's inaugural presidential address to Congress in 1929, quoted in M.J. Akbar, *Nehru*, Penguin, 1989, p. 466.**

*I must frankly confess that I am a socialist and a republican and am no believer in kings and princes, or in the order which produces the modern kings of industry who have greater power over the lives and fortunes of men than even the kings of old and whose methods are as predatory as those of the old feudal aristocracy.*

What does Source A tell us about Nehru's desire for the future of India?

The 1931 Congress at Karachi adopted twenty Fundamental Rights, including secularism, trade union rights and a basic socialist principle: state (that is, government) control of key industries and mineral resources (often termed nationalisation).

Nehru was a leader of the Congress Socialist Party, along with Bose, and both were indulged as 'young radicals' (young hooligans, see page 49) by the leadership. In turn, they encouraged Communists, whose party was banned by the British, to join Congress and strengthen its left wing. When finally Bose became Congress president in 1938, he formed a National Planning Committee with Nehru as chairman. The objective was to improve the economy and people's standard of living, largely through government-led industrialisation. Because of the war and Nehru's imprisonment, this committee only finally completed its projected business in 1945. (By then, Bose had fought with the Japanese and been killed, see page 75.) On formation of the interim government of 1946, Nehru immediately set up a planning advisory board but this in turn was overwhelmed by the tragic chaos of partition.

In 1948 the independent Indian government passed its first industrial policy resolution approving complete state control of armaments manufacture, atomic (nuclear) energy and railways, and major influence over coal, steel, mining, shipbuilding, aircraft and communications. The 1950 republican constitution included principles of state economic policy. Finally, in 1952, Nehru's first Indian Five-Year Plan was approved.

## The first Five-Year Plan 1952

The content was not revolutionary; in fact, the plan mainly gathered together projects already underway to rebuild the economy after the war and partition and to control inflation and food shortages. The main investment would be in the public sector (not-for-profit), whereas private sector businesses (for profit) would need government licences to expand.

The most significant success was in the field of agricultural production. The plan included investment in machinery and irrigation but also, true to socialist principles, radical land reform. It was discovered that the poorest 60 per cent of the population owned only eight per cent of the land. So, the *zamindar* landlord class was abolished and peasant cooperatives were supported. Village councils (*panchayats*) were empowered to discuss and make local improvements. In time, food production rose by twenty per cent, national income by eighteen per cent, per capita (personal) income by eleven per cent and consumption by nine per cent.

Buoyed by such success, preparations were made in 1956 for a second Five-Year Plan. At the Congress meeting in Avadi, 300,000 delegates gathered to hear Nehru declare that the peaceful defeat of the British Empire would be surpassed by the peaceful defeat of poverty and economic inequality. Indian socialism would succeed without revolutionary violence.

State control of strategic industries was extended to the following industries:

- iron and steel making
- heavy casting, forging
- heavy machinery and machine tool production
- mining and oil production
- metal ore processing
- aircraft production
- shipbuilding
- electrical power stations and distribution
- communications.

However, the huge investment costs in industry meant a drastic reduction in investment in agriculture. Nehru hoped that greater efficiency from human labour would meet the need for greater food production. In fact, production fell so the price of food increased dramatically and when the 1957 monsoon rains failed, the country faced a dangerous situation. Nehru was forced to buy food from the USA, Australia and neighbouring countries in south-east Asia which had surplus to sell.

Notwithstanding this setback, Nehru had established an Indian **great leap forward**, firmly placing India on the path towards a modern society. India is set to become one of the world's economic superpowers during the present century.

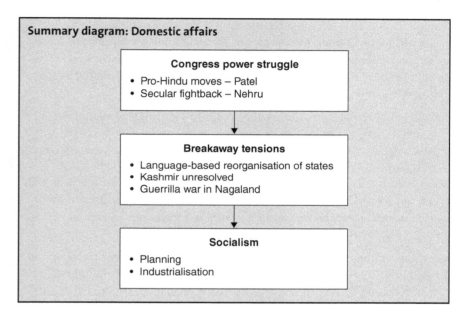

Summary diagram: Domestic affairs

**Congress power struggle**
- Pro-Hindu moves – Patel
- Secular fightback – Nehru

↓

**Breakaway tensions**
- Language-based reorganisation of states
- Kashmir unresolved
- Guerrilla war in Nagaland

↓

**Socialism**
- Planning
- Industrialisation

**KEY TERMS**

**Great leap forward** Communist Chinese campaign for rapid industrialisation as part of China's second Five-Year Plan 1958–62.

**Cold War** A long-running tension with potential to become hot (nuclear) war.

**NATO** North Atlantic Treaty Organisation. A Western military alliance.

**Warsaw Pact** A military alliance of Communist-controlled East European states.

*Pax Americana* Latin phrase modelled on the enforced peace of the Roman Empire.

**Proxy** A substitute for the real thing.

# 2 International relations

▶ *How successful were Nehru's international policies?*

The Western Allies of the Second World War became suspicious opponents in the **Cold War**. Winston Churchill described the situation as though an iron curtain had descended across Europe, partitioning Germany itself and dividing the Continent into spheres defended by the new **NATO** in the West and the **Warsaw Pact** in the East. Britain's pre-war dominance was completely overshadowed by the USA's economic and military power. Britain was victorious but impoverished. US President Truman declared a *Pax Americana* to replace *Pax Britannica*. Across the globe, the superpowers of the modern world, the USA and the Soviet Union, secured new allies in countless **proxy** conflicts.

## Tension on the subcontinent

### Pakistan

In the subcontinent, even before final independence, it had been clear that Britain and the USA saw Pakistan as much more likely to be an ally than an

India led by Nehru, whose socialism had been developed by his admiration of the Soviet Union. Pakistan's relative weakness economically and militarily would mean that it would be grateful for and eventually dependent on Western support. For example, there were plans to develop a huge military base at the port of Karachi in Pakistan.

In 1947 Mountbatten had exploited Indian anxiety about future support for Pakistan to persuade V.P. Menon (see page 132) to agree to Indian Dominion status within the Commonwealth as a means of keeping some British and US support. Relations between India and Pakistan have been tense since independence, sometimes flaring into open war. However, this did not happen during the Nehru years: Nehru worked hard to avoid it.

Following India's declaration of republic status in 1950, there were massacres of Hindus in East Pakistan, leading to mass migrations over the border to India. Patel urged an Indian military invasion to bring order. Nehru's preferred (Gandhian) strategy was to invite the Pakistani prime minister, Liaquat Ali Khan, to tour the region with him to calm things down. There was no response. When Indian Hindus in Calcutta took reprisals on Muslims, Nehru imposed martial law and prepared the army for possible intervention in Pakistan, warning Pakistan through communication with Britain.

Khan flew to India for talks in April 1950, leading to the so-called Nehru–Liaquat Pact. This promised complete equality and protection of minority communities, which Nehru as a dedicated critic of religious communal politics could commit to. However, just one month later Khan made a state visit to the USA and declared: 'There is no room here for theocracy, for Islam stands for freedom of conscience, condemns coercion, has no priesthood and abhors the caste system.'

This appeared to be a taunt to the secularist Nehru that Pakistan was more socially advanced. Patel denounced the comment as an immediate breach of the spirit of the pact. What was even more significant, however, was Khan's open invitation to the USA to guarantee protection of Pakistani territory, suggesting that Pakistan would welcome US military support and provide US and British access to its northern regions bordering Soviet Russia and Communist China.

## The Indo-Pak Wars

There was outright war in 1965 and again in 1971 when an internal revolt in East Pakistan, supported by India, led to the creation of independent Bangladesh. Since 1984 Indian and Pakistani troops have skirmished on the Siachen Glacier, the highest battlefield in the world, where more troops have died of the cold than of the conflict.

## Portuguese Goa

Global strategy also played its part in the messy affair of Goa which, along with Daman and Diu, had remained a Portuguese colony at independence. The USA was keen to develop Goa as a military base and supported continued Portuguese control, despite Portugal itself still being controlled by a fascist dictator, Salazar. Britain too said that it would have to honour treaties with Portugal. (The 1373 Anglo-Portuguese Treaty of 'perpetual friendship' is the oldest active treaty in the world and was part of the reason for Portugal remaining neutral in the Second World War, despite Salazar.)

The colony was a thorn in India's side but Nehru was determined that if the subcontinent could become independent without formal conflict (partition massacres being intercommunal rather than international), then such a small problem should also be solved peacefully through patient dialogue.

This patience was severely tested in 1955 when a mass *satyagraha* (see page 39) deliberately crossed the border into Goa in a peaceful invasion. Portuguese Goan troops opened fire on the protesters, killing many. There were further border incidents over the next few years, with Pakistan supporting Portugal and the Soviet Union supporting India. Meanwhile, in Africa there were full-scale wars of independence in Portuguese colonial countries (for example, Mozambique) which perhaps moved Nehru towards confrontation. In 1961, sensing escalation, the USA proposed six months of negotiations but Nehru's patience had snapped and he ordered an Indian attack. Portugal had ordered its colony to resist determinedly but the governor-general, de Silva, humanely avoided a bloodbath by surrendering immediately. For his part, Nehru acknowledged that he had, in the end, set aside his principles in order to finally rid the subcontinent of European colonial possessions.

## The non-aligned movement

On the wider global stage, however, Nehru's principles are arguably his greatest personal legacy. He not only steered a course for India between the Cold War superpowers, but also articulated a vision for many countries, notably those freeing themselves from former colonial powers. This loose collection of states became known as the non-aligned movement. Its three great leaders were Nehru, President Tito of Yugoslavia and President Nasser of Egypt.

Tito was a former leader of the Communist resistance against the Nazis. He stunned the world, and the Soviet leader Stalin in particular, by refusing to join the Warsaw Pact in order to lead an independent Communist European state. Nasser, an army general, had come to power in a military coup against King Farouk in 1952 and had spectacularly defeated an attempt by Britain, France and Israel to seize control of the Suez Canal in 1956. The USA had not been consulted, and denounced it as a disastrous military adventure, dooming it to failure and causing the resignation of the British prime minister, Anthony Eden, whereas Nehru's support for Egypt in the crisis increased admiration for India in the Muslim Arab world, to the irritation of Pakistan.

## Pancha sheela

Nehru's views of international relations were expressed in the Five Principles of Coexistence, otherwise known as the *Pancha sheela* ('five virtues') Treaty. The five principles were as follows:

- Respect for sovereignty, particularly of small, newly independent states.
- Non-aggression in resolution of disputes.
- Non-interference in internal affairs.
- Equality of treatment.
- Peaceful coexistence.

For Nehru, these values were an extension of his nationalist ambitions for economic equality and political freedom as the conditions for social peace. He recognised that these were ideals but in another memorable Nehruvian phrase called them 'the realism of tomorrow'. In the interim government of 1946 he had ensured that he took responsibility for external affairs and Commonwealth relations.

> **SOURCE B**
>
> **From a foreign policy statement of Nehru in 1946, quoted in M.J. Akbar, *Nehru*, Penguin, 1989, p. 484.**
>
> *We propose, as far as possible, to keep away from the power politics of groups, aligned against one another, which have led in the past to world war and which may again lead to disasters on an even vaster scale. We believe that peace and freedom are indivisible and the denial of freedom anywhere must endanger freedom elsewhere and lead to conflict and war. We are particularly interested in the emancipation of colonial and dependent countries and peoples, and in the recognition in theory and practice of equal opportunity for all races … We seek no dominion over others and we claim no privileged position over other peoples. But we do claim equal and honourable treatment for our people wherever they may go and we cannot accept any discrimination against them.*

**?** Identify the elements of the *Pancha sheela* in Source B.

Nehru had convened the first Asian Relations Conference in 1947, promoting a new sense of independent Asian self-confidence. He declared: 'We do not intend to be the playthings of others.' This irritated the USA but also provoked criticism from the Soviet Union and China that India was in fact still a Western puppet because it remained in the Commonwealth (of former British colonies).

The two high points of the non-aligned movement were the **Bandung** Conference of 1955 and the anti-nuclear statement of 1961. Bandung brought together leaders from across not only Asia but also now Africa. The final **communiqué** was a version of the *Pancha sheela,* although it did include the right to self-defence through participation in military alliances.

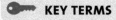 **KEY TERMS**

**Bandung** A city in Java, Indonesia.

**Communiqué** Agreed statement at the end of a political conference, but not a treaty.

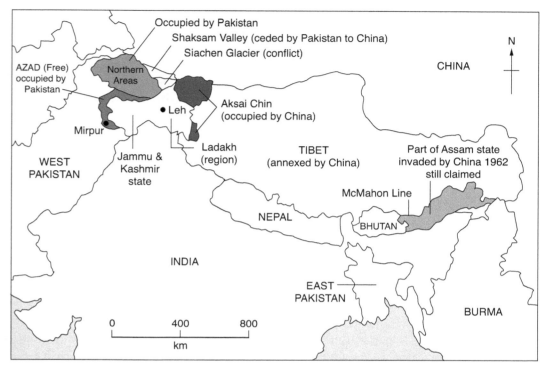

**Figure 7.2** Areas of conflict along India's northern borders.

The 1961 condemnation of potential nuclear war, issued by Nehru, Nasser and Tito in Belgrade, was the most formal commitment of non-alignment.

Nehru visited both the USA and the Soviet Union. In the former, he was received with suspicion of Communist sympathies and responded with condescension for the younger President Kennedy. He was more charming towards the latter, sending two baby elephants for Moscow zoo. He secured Soviet investment for a massive steel plant, which so alarmed the USA and Europe that they followed suit despite previous refusals to invest.

The Korean War of 1950–3 was a test of non-alignment. India supported the United Nations resolution which declared the aggressor to be the Communist North Koreans, but would not support war as the solution. India played a role as an intermediary between China, the superpower behind the North Korean strategy, and the United Nations defending the South, resulting in prisoner exchanges (delayed because northern prisoners did not want to be sent back). Nehru was to find China even more difficult as a direct opponent.

## The Chinese incursion

The roots of the hostilities between India and China lie in British attempts to clarify the boundaries of the Empire. The so-called Durand Line of 1893 aimed to reduce the need for dangerous British advances into Afghanistan. In 1913 the foreign secretary (of the Raj government), Sir Henry McMahon, had brokered an agreement among British India, Russia, China and Tibet concerning the border across the whole of the north of the subcontinent – the McMahon Line – and, at the same time, recognising Tibet as an autonomous state. However, the Chinese delegate's agreement was revoked by the Chinese government and a subsequent revision was only agreed with the Tibetan representative.

In 1949 the new Communist People's Republic of China announced that it regarded Tibet as part of China and would annex it. In October 1950, while the world was watching the escalation of the Korean War, Chinese troops occupied Tibet. It was over in five days and before the world knew anything of it. The Indians were horrified. Although Patel warned that the Chinese were clearly prepared to ignore all treaty recognitions, Nehru wanted to pursue peaceful negotiations in line with *Pancha sheela*, while declaring that the McMahon Line was the border of independent India. India took the precaution of moving troops up to its side of the McMahon Line and the Chinese prime minister, Zhou Enlai, announced that there was no dispute over the border. The Indian government believed that the right approach had been adopted and Nehru was reluctant to push the matter on towards an actual agreement. Nehru's biographer, M.J. Akbar, speculates that Nehru may have behaved over-optimistically out of reluctance to confront the Chinese and reinforce a popular stereotype that they were an untrustworthy people. This does not, however, justify the Indian government's recognition in 1954 of Chinese control of Tibet without any mention of the McMahon Line.

In July 1954, just days after a visit to India by Zhou Enlai, China upped the stakes by protesting at Indian troops at Barahoti, which it claimed was Chinese territory. Nehru said that the Chinese were mistaken. In October he visited China and raised the matter. Zhou Enlai smoothed matters by 'admitting' that their maps must be out of date. Accordingly, the Survey of India published new maps showing the historic borderline. At the Bandung Conference, Zhou Enlai again dismissed the growing number of border incidents as minor matters.

## Aksai Chin

In October 1957 India discovered that for the past year and a half the Chinese had been building a strategic road across the Aksai Chin region, a clearly marked, but completely uninhabited, part of India. The road facilitated increasing troop provocations and Chinese fighter aircraft flew over Ladakh with impunity. By contrast, Indian reinforcements to the Ladakhi capital, Leh, still had to use mule transport.

Finally, in 1959, the Chinese declared a full border dispute, denying that any agreements had ever been made and, in any case, rejecting them as out of date British imperial negotiations. They declared that 'the time was now ripe for settlement of the issues' (because the **facts on the ground** were in their favour).

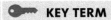 **KEY TERM**

**Facts on the ground**
A political acknowledgement that illegal occupation cannot be reversed.

Nehru agreed to a ceasefire but not to the annexation of Aksai Chin. China simply went a step further, pushing troops as far as Leh in October 1959.

**SOURCE C**

**Mules carrying ammunition over a mountain pass during the conflict between China and India, November 1962.**

What does the photo in Source C of an Indian military mule train reveal about the challenges of combat in the Himalayas?

The Indians faced a huge challenge in responding. The defence minister, Krishna Menon, a key Nehru supporter, had reduced the size of the armed forces in line with the Nehruvian commitment to non-aggression. Forces were already committed to the Nagaland guerrilla war and defence against Pakistan. War in the sacred Himalayas had not been imagined. There were forced resignations, although Menon clung on. Nehru demanded stronger border patrols with more soldiers in reserve.

On 8 September 1962, while the world was watching the unfolding **Cuban Missile Crisis** and Nehru was in London, the Chinese swarmed across the McMahon Line, overwhelming the patrols. It was discovered that the reserves had not even been put in place. On 20 October a full invasion took place, seizing 30,000 square kilometres of Indian territory in both the north-west and north-east (Assam).

To Nehru's embarrassment, the non-aligned movement refused to condemn China, whereas the USA and Britain supported India. When President Kennedy, who had just faced down the Russians over Cuba, warned that the USA was watching closely, the Chinese finally stopped. On 21 November a ceasefire was announced and the Chinese handed back 15,000 square kilometres of territory. To this day they retain control of Aksai Chin and lay claim to a large area in the north-east. They had what they wanted, not least the humiliation of India and

 **KEY TERM**

**Cuban Missile Crisis** The USA discovered that Soviet missiles were to be installed on Cuba and ordered their removal. There were several days of severe tension.

the hero of the non-aligned movement. In the public's perception, it was no coincidence that Nehru's health deteriorated from April 1962. He died two years later.

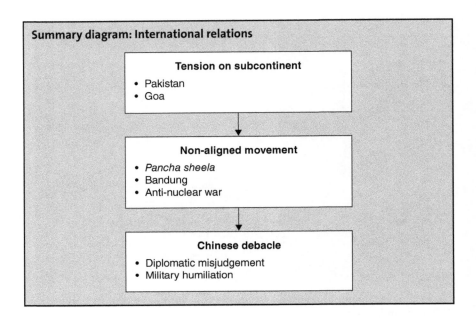

**Summary diagram: International relations**

**Tension on subcontinent**
- Pakistan
- Goa

**Non-aligned movement**
- *Pancha sheela*
- Bandung
- Anti-nuclear war

**Chinese debacle**
- Diplomatic misjudgement
- Military humiliation

## Chapter summary

Nehru was a skilful leader not just of a movement but of the government of a new country. Unlike Gandhi who could not adjust to the political compromises and disappointments of actually governing, Nehru did achieve practical success, particularly in speeding up the industrialisation of India through government direction and investment. However, in many ways, his greatest achievements were, like Gandhi's, inspirational and visionary. As a committed secularist, he resisted efforts to make Congress a pro-Hindu organisation and to make India a religious state facing Muslim Pakistan. He led forcefully towards a socialist planned economy, designed to benefit the whole population. His great weakness was Kashmir and he was outmanoeuvred by the Chinese, but he avoided the trap and tragedy of war with Pakistan. He was personally associated with the vision of a bloc of developing countries which declined to become the puppets of the capitalist and Communist superpowers.

Refresher questions

Use these questions to remind yourself of the key material covered in this chapter.

1  What struggles did Nehru face in and outside Congress?
2  How did Nehru emerge successful?
3  What were the key movements for internal reorganisation in India?
4  Why is the Kashmir problem unresolved?
5  What was the basis of Nehru's economic policy?
6  What were the key features of the Five-Year Plans?
7  How were tensions with Pakistan dealt with?
8  How did Nehru handle the Goa crisis?
9  What was the distinctive contribution of non-alignment to international affairs?
10  What were the *Pancha sheela*?
11  How did Nehru approach the border problems with China?
12  What happened in Aksai Chin?

 Question practice

**ESSAY QUESTIONS**

1  Evaluate the opportunities and challenges faced by Nehru as prime minister of India.
2  To what extent did Nehru make India a more secular, socialist state?
3  'In India's relations with other powers, Nehru's principles led to failure more than success.' To what extent do you agree with this statement?
4  Compare and contrast the vision and achievements of Gandhi and Nehru.

# Edexcel A level History

## Essay guidance

Edexcel's Paper 2, Option 2F.1: India *c.*1914–1948: The Road to Independence is assessed by an exam comprising two sections:

- Section A tests the depth of your historical knowledge through source analysis (see page 162 for guidance on this).
- Section B requires you to write one essay from a choice of two from your own knowledge.

The following advice relates to Paper 2, Section B. It is relevant to A level and AS level questions. Generally, the AS exam is similar to the A level exam. Both examine the same content and require similar skills; nonetheless, there are differences, which are discussed below.

## Essay skills

In order to get a high grade in Section B of Paper 2 your essay must contain four essential qualities:

- focused analysis
- relevant detail
- supported judgement
- organisation, coherence and clarity.

This section focuses on the following aspects of exam technique:

- understanding the nature of the question
- planning an answer to the question set
- writing a focused introduction
- deploying relevant detail
- writing analytically
- reaching a supported judgement.

## The nature of the question

Section B questions are designed to test the depth of your historical knowledge. Therefore, they can focus on relatively short periods, or single events, or indeed on the whole period from 1914 to 1948. Moreover,

they can focus on different historical processes or 'concepts'. These include:

- cause
- consequence
- change/continuity
- similarity/difference
- significance.

These different question focuses require slightly different approaches:

| Cause | 1 To what extent was the British government responsible for the failure of the Cripps mission? |
|---|---|
| Consequence | 2 To what extent did disagreements among Indian representatives destroy the hopes for the Round Table Conferences? |
| Continuity and change | 3 'The constitutional reforms brought in by the Government of India Act of 1919 failed to satisfy the demands of Indian nationalists.' How far do you agree with this statement? |
| Similarities and differences | 4 'There were significant differences between Congress and the Muslim League concerning the future of India in the period 1919 to 1932.' How far do you agree with this statement? |
| Significance | 5 How significant was the Salt March in achieving Gandhi's objectives for *satyagraha*? |

Some questions include a 'stated factor'. The most common type of stated factor question would ask how far one factor caused something. For example, the first question in the table asks: 'To what extent was the British government responsible for the failure of the Cripps mission?' In this type of question you would be expected to evaluate British government actions (such as their objectives for the mission and how much flexibility was permitted) – the 'stated factor' – compared to other factors, such as Indian reactions and Cripps' own initiatives.

## AS and A level questions

AS level questions are generally similar to A level questions. However, the wording of AS questions will be slightly less complex than the wording of A level questions.

| A level question | AS level question | Differences |
|---|---|---|
| 'Jinnah's political strategy changed profoundly in the years 1937–40.' How far do you agree with this statement? | How far did Jinnah's political strategy change in the years 1937–40? | The AS question asks how big a change there was; the A level question asks you to evaluate whether the changes were to long-term goals or to short-term negotiating tactics. Note that the AS question could be asked at A level with an expectation of assessing consequences as well. |

To achieve the highest level at A level, you will have to deal with the full complexity of the question. For example, if you were dealing with the question about Jinnah's change of strategy you would have to examine whether the changes were temporary and tactical, keeping the same goal, or whether they are evidence of a more permanent change of objective.

## Planning your answer

It is crucial that you understand the focus of the question. Therefore, read the question carefully before you start planning. Check the following:

- The chronological focus: which years should your essay deal with?
- The topic focus: what aspect of your course does the question deal with?

- The conceptual focus: is this a causes, consequences, change/continuity, similarity/difference or significance question?

For example, for question 3 you could point these out as follows:

> 'The constitutional reforms brought in by the Government of India Act[1] of 1919 failed[2] to satisfy the demands of Indian nationalists[3].' How far do you agree with this statement?

1  Topic focus: the Government of India Act 1919.
2  Conceptual focus: continuity/change.
3  Chronological focus: *c.*1909–30 – nationalist demands built up before the Act but might also have been satisfied as the provisions of the Act gradually worked their way into the administration of India in the years following.

Your plan should reflect the task that you have been set. Section B asks you to write an analytical, coherent and well-structured essay from your own knowledge, which reaches a supported conclusion in around 40 minutes.

- To ensure that your essay is coherent and well structured, your essay should comprise a series of paragraphs, each focusing on a different point.
- Your paragraphs should come in a logical order. For example, you could write your paragraphs in order of importance, so you begin with the most important issues and end with the least important.
- In essays where there is a 'stated factor', it is a good idea to start with the stated factor before moving on to the other points.
- To make sure you keep to time, you should aim to write three or four paragraphs plus an introduction and a conclusion.

### The opening paragraph

The opening paragraph should do four main things:

- answer the question directly
- set out your essential argument
- outline the factors or issues that you will discuss
- define key terms used in the question – where necessary.

Different questions require you to define different terms, for example:

| A level question | Key terms |
|---|---|
| How significant was the Salt March in achieving Gandhi's objectives for *satyagraha*? | Here, it is necessary to explain '*satyagraha*'. |
| 'There were significant differences between Congress and the Muslim League concerning the future of India in the period 1919–32.' How far do you agree with this statement? | In this example, it is worth defining Congress and the Muslim League. |

Here's an example introduction in answer to question 5 in the table on page 158: 'How significant was the Salt March in achieving Gandhi's objectives for *satyagraha*?'

*The Salt March was highly significant as a successful example of satyagraha. Gandhi developed the concept of satyagraha and explained it as the 'quiet and irresistible pursuit of truth'* **[1]**. *In practice, this meant taking peaceful action to draw attention to an injustice and, if necessary, suffering a violent reaction from powerful opponents* **[2]**. *Although the Salt March did not actually alter the tax on salt, it achieved the objectives of satyagraha, including provoking the British authorities into an aggressive overreaction which was publicised around the world* **[3]**.

1 The essay starts with a clear answer to the question.
2 The term *satyagraha* is explained specifically and practically.
3 Finally, the essential argument is stated that, although nothing changed, the campaign was a successful *satyagraha* action.

### The opening paragraph: advice

- Don't write more than a couple of sentences on general background knowledge. This is unlikely to focus explicitly on the question.
- After defining key terms, refer back to these definitions when justifying your conclusion.

- The introduction should reflect the rest of the essay. Don't make one argument in your introduction, then make a different argument in the essay.

## Deploying relevant detail

Paper 2 tests the depth of your historical knowledge. Therefore, you will need to deploy historical detail. In the main body of your essay your paragraphs should begin with a clear point, be full of relevant detail and end with explanation or evaluation. A detailed answer might include statistics, proper names, dates and technical terms. For example, if you were writing a paragraph about the Government of India Act 1919, you could show your grasp of the main legal details about dyarchy and the division of powers, and the meaning of dominion status and reserved electorates.

## Writing analytically

The quality of your analysis is one of the key factors that determines the mark you achieve. Writing analytically means clearly showing the relationships between the ideas in your essay. Analysis includes two key skills: explanation and evaluation.

## Explanation

Explanation means giving reasons. An explanatory sentence has three parts:

- a claim: a statement that something is true or false
- a reason: a statement that justifies the claim
- a relationship: a word or phrase that shows the relationship between the claim and the reason.

Imagine you are answering question 1 in the table on page 158: 'To what extent was the British government responsible for the failure of the Cripps mission?'

Your paragraph on Cripps' second objective (minor changes to Indian government during the war) should start with a clear point, which would be supported by reasons. Finally, you would round off the paragraph with some explanation:

*Therefore, Cripps' proposal that the Executive Council should immediately include an Indian* defence minister was[1] one of the reasons for the mission's failure[2] because it provided the British government with an excuse to say that Cripps had gone too far and so to reject the whole mission[3].

1 Claim.
2 Relationship.
3 Reason.

Make sure of the following:

- The reason you give genuinely justifies the claim you have made.
- Your explanation is focused on the question.

## Reaching a supported judgement

Finally, your essay should reach a supported judgement. The obvious place to do this is in the conclusion of your essay. Even so, the judgement should reflect the findings of your essay. The conclusion should present:

- a clear judgement that answers the question
- an evaluation of the evidence that supports the judgement.

Finally, the evaluation should reflect valid criteria.

### Evaluation and criteria

Evaluation means weighing up to reach a judgement. Therefore, evaluation requires you to:

- summarise both sides of the issue
- reach a conclusion that reflects the proper weight of both sides.

So, for question 4 in the table on page 158: ' "There were significant differences between Congress and the Muslim League concerning the future of India in the period 1919–32." How far do you agree with this statement?', the conclusion might look like this:

In conclusion, the evidence shows that over this period the two organisations remained largely in agreement following the Lucknow Pact[1]. However, from the start, Gandhi's direct action campaigns, even though non-violent in intent, were not the style of the educated middle-class members of the Muslim League. As a consequence,

the League was overshadowed by the dynamism of Congress, which attracted an increasing number of members, including Muslims. The Nehru Report is usually seen as the point of divergence but contemporaneous Muslim League proposals were still actually quite similar[2]. The public split occurred at the All Parties Convention of 1928-9 when Jinnah personally argued for keeping the Lucknow agreement. When Congress rejected this, Jinnah made his grander counter-proposal, known as the Fourteen Points, which failed to gather support even from the Muslim League and led to Jinnah's (temporary) abandonment of Indian politics[3]. Therefore, it would be fair to conclude that differences were much less apparent than agreement for most of the period, until the rather abrupt intervention by Jinnah, and even then it was a technical disagreement about voting rather than about the future of India[4].

1 The conclusion starts with a clear signpost that the answer is not going to agree entirely with the statement.
2 The conclusion summarises the evidence over the period, including revisionist views.
3 The conclusion considers the weight of evidence in terms of years (of agreement or disagreement) and how deep the difference was (Jinnah isolated even from his own supporters).
4 The essay ends with a final judgement which refers back to the question wording but is not afraid to come to a slightly different conclusion.

The significant feature of this question is a rather one-sided description that can be challenged on the basis of the evidence, which will have been considered in more detail in the main part of the essay. A confident, well-supported answer can reach a nuanced judgement which does not simply try to prove that the statement is correct.

# Sources guidance

Edexcel's Paper 2, Option 2F.1: India *c.*1914–1948: The Road to Independence is assessed by an exam comprising two sections:

- Section A tests the depth of your historical knowledge through source analysis.
- Section B requires you to write one essay from a choice of two from your own knowledge (see page 158 for guidance on this).

The following advice relates to Paper 2, Section A. It is relevant to A level and AS level questions. Generally, the AS exam is similar to the A level exam. Both examine the same content and require similar skills; nonetheless, there are differences, which are discussed below.

The questions in Paper 2, Section A, are structured differently in the A level and AS exams.

| AS exam | Full A level exam |
|---------|-------------------|
| Section A: contains one compulsory question divided into two parts. Part a) is worth 8 marks. It focuses on the value of a single source for a specific enquiry. Part b) is worth 12 marks. It asks you to weigh the value of a single source for a specific enquiry. Together the two sources will comprise about 350 words. | Section A: contains a single compulsory question worth 20 marks. The question asks you to evaluate the usefulness of two sources for a specific historical enquiry. Together the two sources will comprise about 400 words. |
| Questions will start with the following stems: a) Why is Source 1 valuable to the historian for an enquiry into … ? b) How much weight do you give the evidence of Source 2 for an enquiry into … ? | Questions will start with the following stem: **1** How far could the historian make use of Sources 1 and 2 together to investigate … ? |

## Edexcel style questions

### AS style question

Study Sources 1 and 2 before you answer this question.

a) Why is Source 1 valuable to the historian for an enquiry into the British government's thinking on the difficulties of Indian constitutional reform in the years 1919–35? Explain your answer using the source, the information given about it and your own knowledge of the historical context.

b) How much weight do you give the evidence of Source 2 for an enquiry into the change from British district officers to Indian politicians in the administration of India in the years 1919–35? Explain your answer using the source, the information given about it and your own knowledge of the historical context.

### A level style question

Study Sources 3 and 4 (page 164) before you answer this question.

How far could the historian make use of Sources 3 and 4 together to investigate the growing ineffectiveness of legal punishment in dealing with the nationalist movement?

Explain your answer using both sources, the information given about them and your own knowledge of the historical context.

## Sources 1–4

### SOURCE 1

**From The Report on Indian Constitutional Reforms (1918) (the Montagu–Chelmsford Report), quoted in C.H. Philips, editor, with H.L. Singh and B.N. Pandey,** *The Evolution of India and Pakistan 1858 to 1947: Select Documents,* **Oxford University Press, 1962.**

*Division by creeds and classes means the creation of political camps organised against each other, and teaches men to think as partisans and not as citizens; and it is difficult to see how the change from this system to national representation is ever to occur. The British Government is often accused of dividing men in order to govern them. But if it unnecessarily divides them at the very moment when it professes to start them on the road to governing themselves, it will find it difficult to meet the charge of being hypocritical or short-sighted.*

*A minority which is given special representation owing to its weak and backward state, is positively encouraged to settle down into a feeling of satisfied security;*

*We regard any system of communal electorates, therefore, as a very serious hindrance to the development of the self-governing principle … At the same time we must face the hard facts. The Muhammadans [Muslims] were given special representation with separate electorates in 1909 [Indian Councils Act ] … Much as we regret the necessity, we are convinced that so far as the Muhammadans at all events are concerned the present system must be maintained until conditions alter, even at the price of slower progress towards the realisation of a common citizenship.*

### SOURCE 2

**From Roland Hunt and John Harrison,** *The District Officer in India, 1930–1947,* **Scolar Press, 1980.**

*Under varying degrees of official supervision, local politicians had also taken charge of the self-governing municipalities administering the town and the district boards in the rural areas. The district officer had to learn to share power with the politician. Moreover, the civil service itself was changing: since 1924 there had been no British recruitment to the professional and technical All-India services except the police, and more Indians were entering the Indian Civil Service …*

*[C.S.] Venkatachar [district officer in United Provinces and Indian Political Service 1922–60] argues that an irreversible shift of power occurred between 1919 and 1935: 'The politics of mediation between the people and the government had shifted … The politician now stood forward as the mediator and had displaced the district officer … The decline in the influence of the [district officer's] position was visible'.*

## SOURCE 3

**From Gandhi's final address to the judge (Broomfield) at his trial, quoted in C.H. Philips, editor, with H.L. Singh and B.N. Pandey, *The Evolution of India and Pakistan 1858 to 1947: Select Documents*, Oxford University Press, 1962.**

*In my humble opinion, non-cooperation with evil is as much a duty as is co-operation with good ... I am here, therefore, to invite and submit cheerfully to the highest penalty that can be inflicted upon me for what in law is a deliberate crime and what appears to me to be the highest duty of a citizen. The only course open to you, the Judge, is either to resign your post and thus dissociate yourself from evil, if you feel that the law you are called upon to administer is an evil and that in reality I am innocent; or to inflict on me the severest penalty if you believe that the system and the law you are assisting to administer are good.*

## SOURCE 4

**From the judgement by Broomfield, 18 March 1922, quoted in C.H. Philips, editor, with H.L. Singh and B.N. Pandey, *The Evolution of India and Pakistan 1858 to 1947: Select Documents*, Oxford University Press, 1962.**

*There are probably few people in India, who do not sincerely regret that you should have made it impossible for any government to leave you at liberty. But it is so. I am trying to balance what is due to you against what appears to me to be necessary in the interest of the public. [The judge then justifies his sentence by comparison with the sentence passed on Tilak twelve years before.] You will not consider it unreasonable, I think, that you should be classed with Mr Tilak, ... six years in all, which I feel it my duty to pass upon you, and I should like to say in doing so that, if the course of events in India should make it possible for the Government to reduce the period and release you, no one will be better pleased than I.*

## Understanding the questions

- To answer the question successfully you must understand how the question works.
- The question is written precisely in order to make sure that you understand the task. Each part of the question has a specific meaning.
- You must use the source, the information given about the source and your own knowledge of the historical context when answering the question.

## Understanding the AS question

a) Why is Source 1 valuable to the historian for an enquiry into[1] the British government's thinking on the difficulties of Indian constitutional reform in the years 1919–35[2]?

Explain your answer using the source, the information given about it and your own knowledge of the historical context.

1 You must focus on the reasons why the source could be helpful to a historian. Indeed, you can get maximum marks without considering the source's limitations.

2 The final part of the question focuses on a specific topic that a historian might investigate. In this case: 'the British government's thinking on the difficulties of Indian constitutional reform in the years 1919–35'.

b) How much weight do you give the evidence of Source 2 for an enquiry into[1] the change from British district officers to Indian politicians[2] in the administration of India in the years 1919–35[3]?

Explain your answer using the source, the information given about it and your own knowledge of the historical context.

1 This question focuses on evaluating the extent to which the source contains evidence. Therefore, you must consider the ways in which the source is valuable and the limitations of the source.

2 This is the essence of the task: you must focus on what a historian could legitimately conclude from studying this source.

3 This is the specific topic that you are considering the source for: evidence of 'change from British district officers to Indian politicians in the administration of India in the years 1919–35'.

### Understanding the A level question

How far[1] could the historian make use of Sources 3 and 4[2] together[3] to investigate the growing ineffectiveness of legal punishment in dealing with the nationalist movement[4]?

Explain your answer using both sources, the information given about them and your own knowledge of the historical context[5].

1 You must evaluate the extent of something, rather than giving a simple 'yes' or 'no' answer.

2 This is the essence of the task: you must focus on what a historian could legitimately conclude from studying these sources.

3 You must examine the sources as a pair and make a judgement about both sources, rather than simply making separate judgements about each source.

4 The final part of the question focuses on a specific topic that a historian might investigate. In this case: 'the growing ineffectiveness of legal punishment in dealing with the nationalist movement'.

5 This instruction lists the resources you should use: the sources, the information given about the sources and your own knowledge of the historical context that you have learnt during the course.

## Source skills

Generally, Section A of Paper 2 tests your ability to evaluate source material. More specifically, the sources presented in Section A will be taken from the period that you have studied: 1914–48, or be written by people who witnessed these events. Your job is to analyse the sources by reading them in the context of the values and assumptions of the society and period that produced them.

Examiners will mark your work by focusing on the extent to which you are able to:

- Interpret and analyse source material:
  - At a basic level, this means you can understand the sources and select, copy, paraphrase and summarise the source or sources to help answer the question.
  - At a higher level, your interpretation of the sources includes the ability to explain, analyse and make inferences based on the sources.
  - At the highest levels, you will be expected to analyse the source in a sophisticated way. This includes the ability to distinguish between information, opinions and arguments contained in the sources.
- Deploy knowledge of historical context in relation to the sources:
  - At a basic level, this means the ability to link the sources to your knowledge of the context in which the source was written, using this knowledge to expand or support the information contained in the sources.
  - At a higher level, you will be able to use your contextual knowledge to make inferences, and to expand, support or challenge the details mentioned in the sources.
  - At the highest levels, you will be able to examine the value and limits of the material contained in the sources by interpreting the sources in the context of the values and assumptions of the society that produced them.
- Evaluate the usefulness and weight of the source material:
  - At a basic level, evaluation of the source will be based on simplistic criteria about reliability and bias.
  - At a higher level, evaluation of the source will be based on the nature and purpose of the source.
  - At the highest levels, evaluation of the source will be based on a valid criterion that is justified in the course of the essay. You will also be able to distinguish between the value of different aspects of the sources.

Make sure your source evaluation is sophisticated. Avoid crude statements about bias, and avoid simplistic assumptions such as that a source written immediately after an event is reliable, whereas a source written years later is unreliable.

Try to see things through the eyes of the writer:

- How does the writer understand the world?
- What assumptions does the writer have?
- Who is the writer trying to influence?
- What views is the writer trying to challenge?

## Basic skill: comprehension

The most basic source skill is comprehension: understanding what the sources mean. There are a variety of techniques that you can use to aid comprehension. For example, you could read the sources included in this book and in past papers:

- Read the sources out loud.
- Look up any words that you don't understand and make a glossary.
- Make flash cards containing brief biographies of the writers of the sources.

You can demonstrate comprehension by copying, paraphrasing and summarising the sources. However, keep this to the minimum as comprehension is a low-level skill and you need to leave room for higher-level skills.

## Advanced skill: contextualising the sources

First, to analyse the sources correctly you need to understand them in the context in which they were written. People involved in the independence movement and in responding to it legally and politically were making momentous, and sometimes urgent, decisions without knowing the consequences (which later historians can evaluate carefully and without risk to their safety). The sources reflect this. Your job is to understand the values and assumptions behind the source.

- One way of contextualising the sources is to consider the nature, origins and purpose of the sources. However, this can lead to formulaic responses.
- An alternative is to consider two levels of context. First, you should establish the general context. In this case, Sources 1 and 2 refer to a period in

which Gandhi was causing extreme provocation to the government and apparently completely without fear of punishment. Second, you can look for specific references to contemporary events or debates in the sources. For example:

*Sources 3 and 4 both relate to Gandhi and the period of civil disobedience. Gandhi makes an immediate reference to non-cooperation, the term adopted by the protesters. The term emphasises an absence of aggression and the potential weakness of the authorities in needing co-operation. Gandhi then brings in a moral term, evil, which reflects the combination of the spiritual and the political in his philosophy of satyagraha. So, instead of defending himself as innocent, Gandhi 'cheerfully' (Source 3) admits his guilt by turning it into a moral duty and accusing the judge of acting for evil. Because the opposite of evil is often regarded as innocence, Gandhi is saying he is guilty and innocent at the same time! In response, the judge appears to admit the trap which Gandhi has set. In particular, the phrase 'what is due to you' (Source 4) is contrasted with 'necessary in the interest of the public'. If the second phrase implies imprisonment, then the first might imply some recognition of Gandhi's honourable motives. The judge refers to the prison term of Tilak, an earlier nationalist leader, in order to justify the six-year sentence, but this also perhaps recognises that putting Gandhi in prison as the law demands will only strengthen his leadership.*

## Use context to make judgements

- Start by establishing the general context of the source:
  - Ask yourself: what was going on at the time when the source was written, or the time of the events described in the source?
  - What are the key debates that the source might be contributing to?
- Next, look for key words and phrases that establish the specific context. Does the source

refer to specific people, events or books that might be important?
- Make sure your contextualisation focuses on the question.
- Use the context when evaluating the usefulness and limitations of the source.

For example:

Source 3 is valuable to a historian investigating the growing ineffectiveness of the legal process and punishment in dealing with the nationalist movement because it shows how the campaigners were prepared to use their trials to promote their political views and even turn them into accusations against the authorities. Moreover, the force of the punishment was neutralised by the accepting attitude of the campaigners. Although he will be found guilty, Gandhi's tone is mocking and triumphant. Source 4 is valuable because it shows the difficulties of the legal authorities. They knew that what they were required to do would be counter-productive. There is a feeling that the judge recognises the intellectual and spiritual stature of Gandhi and hopes he will be quickly released. Gandhi has outwitted him and he almost asks forgiveness for being unable to make a different decision. It is an admission of eventual defeat.

# Glossary of terms

**Accession**   The process of peacefully merging into a larger country.

**Ahimsa**   Literal meaning is non-violence.

**Anarchic**   Without structure, tending towards political chaos.

**Annexation**   Forced but peaceful conquest of territory.

**Ashram**   Small religious, often farming, community.

**Babu**   Bengali term for clerk.

**Bandung**   A city in Java, Indonesia.

**Besieged**   Surrounded by the enemy but typically within a defensible fortification, creating a long stand-off.

**Bolshevik**   The group that emerged as leaders of the Russian Revolution.

**Cartographical**   Relating to maps.

**Caste**   A rigid public social division. Derived from a Portuguese word. The English word outcast is related.

**Censure**   A formal political reprimand.

**Cold War**   A long-running tension with potential to become hot (nuclear) war.

**Communal**   Relating to religious groups in India.

**Communiqué**   Agreed statement at the end of a political conference, but not a treaty.

**Communist**   The political philosophy of a supposed classless society with workers in power; ideology of the Soviet Union.

**Congress**   Originally a word for a large meeting, later the name of the political party itself.

**Constituent assembly**   A parliament with the sole task of designing a constitution.

**Contiguous**   A formal term for touching or adjoining.

**Court-martialled**   Punished by a military court for breach of army regulations, desertion and so on.

**Cuban Missile Crisis**   The USA discovered that Soviet missiles were to be installed on Cuba and ordered their removal. There were several days of severe tension.

**Defence of the Realm Act**   British emergency law passed four days after the declaration of war, creating censorship and prohibiting certain activities (including all-day pub opening hours).

**Demobilised**   Released from the armed forces (also called demobbed).

**Dhoti**   Loin cloth.

**District**   A formal subdivision of a province.

**Divide and rule**   Imperialist strategy, from Romans onward, of provoking enmities to prevent subject groups uniting in opposition.

**Dominion status**   A category of self-government within the British Empire denoting a full nation.

**Durbar**   Imperial celebration.

**Dyarchy**   Obscure term from classical Greek meaning two-part power.

**Excise**   A tax on goods made inside the country.

**Facts on the ground**   A political acknowledgement that illegal occupation cannot be reversed.

**Federal**   Government with considerable regional powers.

**Federation**   A national political grouping of regions with substantial autonomy.

**For the duration**   Became a common phrase to describe the unknown length of the war.

**Fourteen Points**   US President Wilson's post-war principles of international policy.

**Franchise**   The conditions making people eligible to vote.

**Front-bench position**   A post in the opposition party shadowing an actual government minister.

**Ghadr**   Translates as mutiny.

**Great leap forward**   Communist Chinese campaign for rapid industrialisation as part of China's second Five-Year Plan 1958–62.

**Gurdwara**   Sikh temple.

**Harijans**   Translates as sons of god, considered by others at the time as a rather patronising term, to evoke pity perhaps.

**Hartal**   Translates as strike action, refusal to work.

**Hindustan**   Literally the land beyond the Indus (coming from the west) – an Arab or Mughal perspective.

**Home affairs**   Government department for law, order and justice.

**Interned**   Imprisoned without trial.

**Jatha**   A squad.

**Khadi**   Home-spun cloth or clothing.

**Khilafat** Campaign to protect the last link with the medieval caliphs (from which the name derives), meaning deputies of the Prophet Muhammad and leaders of the global Muslim community.

**Mahasabha** Translates as great association.

**Mandated** Instructed by a political organisation or authority.

**Martial law** Military government, where the army imposes its own rules and suspends civil courts and justice.

**Mesopotamia** The Middle East, especially what is now Iraq, from the Greek for 'between rivers' (the Tigris and Euphrates in Iraq).

**NATO** North Atlantic Treaty Organisation. A Western military alliance.

**Neo-imperialist** A strategy of reimposing an imperial-style control, perhaps through economic power rather than military force.

**North West Frontier Province** One of the eleven British provinces of the Raj, adjoining Afghanistan and close to Russia (across the Hindu Kush mountains).

**Orders-in-council** Legislation approved by a viceroy without full parliamentary scrutiny.

**Ottoman Empire** Islamic Empire of the Middle East and modern Turkey.

**Pacifism** Refusal to fight in wartime.

**Pact** An agreement between political groups or states.

**Panchayat** Assembly (originally of five village elders).

**Pandemic** Global epidemic.

**Paramount power** A diplomatic term for the most powerful force, often an occupying army.

**Paramountcy** Being most important or supreme.

**Parsi** Ancient Iranian religion.

**Partition** The formal division of a state or province.

**Paternalistic** The caring but superior attitude of a parent (specifically a father) who knows best.

**Pax Americana** Latin phrase modelled on the enforced peace of the Roman Empire.

**Plebiscite** A vote of the whole population on constitutional issues.

**Plenipotentiary powers** The capacity to make decisions without approval from government.

**Polytheistic** A religion with many gods and goddesses.

**Proxy** A substitute for the real thing.

**Punjab** A fertile and densely populated region in the north-west, with its own language and culture but now split between India and Pakistan. The name comes from *panch* (five) *ab* (rivers), so often it is also written Panjab.

**Qur'an** The Muslim holy book.

**R.I.** *Rex Imperator,* Latin for King-Emperor.

**Realpolitik** A term for hard-headed pragmatism, borrowed from the German language.

**Round table conference** A meeting of all parties with all opinions equally considered.

**Rupee** The currency of India.

**Ruritanian** From an imaginary place of intrigue and romance.

**Sadhu** Hindu holy man.

**Satyagraha** Translates as truth-force, a term coined by Gandhi to describe non-violent protest.

**Secession** The formal breakaway of one part of a country.

**Secular** Public, non-religious affairs.

**Seditious** Encouraging overthrow of a government.

**Sepoy** An Indian soldier.

**Simla** Pronounced Shimla, summer capital of British India, high in the cool of the mountains.

**Sultan** Muslim Arabic term indicating a regional political and religious leader – in this case the Ottoman emperor – but not claiming to be the supreme caliph.

**Surety** A deposit lost in the event of breaking the law.

**Swadesh** A campaign not to buy something – known as a boycott in English.

**Swaraj** Translates as self-rule.

**Theocratic** A political structure based on religious elites.

**Ulster** Province in the north of Ireland which chose to remain fully British in 1922 when the Irish Free State was created as a Dominion.

**Viceroy** The deputy for a monarch.

**Warsaw Pact** A military alliance of Communist-controlled East European states.

**White man's burden** The perceived duty of white-ruled nations to govern so-called inferior races and countries.

**White paper** A firm set of proposals for legislation.

**Zamindar** A landowner taking rent from peasant farmers.

# Further reading

## Books of overall relevance

P. French, *Liberty or Death: India's Journey to Independence and Division* (Flamingo, 1997)
If you only buy or read one other book on this topic then choose this. Sharp, lively and irreverent

L. James, *Raj: The Making and Unmaking of British India* (Little, Brown, 1997)
Comprehensive history of the English and British in power with interesting diversions into cultural aspects

J. Keay, *India* (HarperCollins, 2000)
A full survey from prehistory to the present day. Very readable sweep

M. Misra, *Vishnu's Crowded Temple India since the Great Rebellion* (Allen Lane, 2007)
Recent and readable narrative survey from the mutiny to the present

## Chapter 1

C.C. Eldridge, *The Imperial Experience* (Macmillan, 1996)
A study of the rhetoric, literature and popular culture of British imperialism

J. Newsinger, *The Blood Never Dried: A People's History of the British Empire* (Bookmarks, 2006)
Interestingly wide-ranging with short sections on India but usefully asserts the perspective of organised industrial labour (and, needless to say, anti-imperialism)

## Chapter 2

T. Coates, editor, *The Amritsar Massacre* (Tim Coates Editions, 2000)
A contextualised summary of the original Hunter Inquiry report

## Chapter 3

J. Adams, *Gandhi* (Quercus, 2010)
Conventional structure following the political chronology with reflections on Gandhi's life and philosophy

R. Hunt and J. Harrison, *The District Officer in India, 1930–1947* (Scolar Press, 1980)
The final three chapters contain interesting extracts from the memoirs of Raj officials in dealing with the changing politics of India

A. Jalal, *The Sole Spokesman* (Cambridge University Press, 1994)
Scholarly work establishing the revisionist view of Jinnah's strategy

B. Parekh, *Gandhi, A Very Short Introduction* (Oxford University Press, 1997)
Thematically structured, so Gandhi's politics play a small part within his life and philosophy

## Chapter 4

H.V. Hodson, *The Great Divide* (Oxford University Press, 1985)
Classic analytical memoir from one close to the political events

D.N. Panigrahi, *India's Partition: The Story of Imperialism in Retreat* (Routledge, 2004)
Scholarly but pro-Nehru and anti-Jinnah

A. Roy, 'The High Politics of India's Partition: The Revisionist Perspective', in Mushirul Hasan, editor, *India's Partition: Process, Strategy and Mobilisation* (Oxford University Press, 1994)
This chapter usefully summarises the orthodox and revisionist positions. (You may be able to ask for a photocopy of the chapter through your local library inter-library loan system)

## Chapter 5

S. Wolpert, *Shameful Flight* (Oxford University Press, 2006)
Critique of Mountbatten and the British from a world scholar

## Chapter 6

L. Collins and D. Lapierre, *Freedom at Midnight* (HarperCollins, 1997)
Based on interviews with Mountbatten and heavily criticised for a lack of balance

V. Schofield, *Kashmir in Conflict* (I.B. Tauris, 2000)
The key scholarly book on Kashmir in English for many years

P. Shankar Jha, *Kashmir 1947* (Oxford University Press, 1996)
Indian perspective, short but not easily accessible

## Chapter 7

M.J. Akbar, *Nehru: The Making of India* (Viking Penguin, 1988)
Supportive but not uncritical standard biography

Sunil Khilnani, *The Idea of India* (Penguin, 1998)
Takes forward the post-independence story